The Handbook of Infrastructure Investing

The Handbook of Infrastructure Investing

MICHAEL D. UNDERHILL,
EDITOR

WILEY

John Wiley & Sons, Inc.

Published by John Wiley & Sons, Inc., Hoboken, New Jersey.

Published simultaneously in Canada.

For general information on our other products and services or for technical support, please contact our Customer Care Department within the United States at (800) 762-2974, outside the United States at (317) 572-3993 or fax (317) 572-4002.

Wiley also publishes its books in a variety of electronic formats. Some content that appears in print may not be available in electronic formats. For more information about Wiley products, visit our Web site at www.wiley.com.

Library of Congress Cataloging-in-Publication Data:

The handbook of infrastructure investing / Michael Underhill, editor.
  p. cm.
 Includes bibliographical references and index.
 ISBN 978-0-470-24367-1 (cloth)
 1. Infrastructure (Economics)–United States.   I. Underhill, Michael D.
 HC110.C3H36 2010
 332.67′22–dc22
                                        2009050965

Printed in the United States of America

10 9 8 7 6 5 4 3 2 1

The Handbook of Infrastructure Investing

MICHAEL D. UNDERHILL,
EDITOR

WILEY

John Wiley & Sons, Inc.

Library of Congress Cataloging-in-Publication Data:

The handbook of infrastructure investing / Michael Underhill, editor.
   p. cm.
Includes bibliographical references and index.
ISBN 978-0-470-24367-1 (cloth)
1. Infrastructure (Economics)–United States.   I. Underhill, Michael D.
HC110.C3H36 2010
332.67'22–dc22

                                       2009050965

Printed in the United States of America

10   9   8   7   6   5   4   3   2   1

Contents

Acknowledgments

With a grateful heart, I would like to thank my family for all of their love and support. Without our family's steadfast support and encouragement of those closest to us we would not be able to conduct the work that we do in service to the United States in solving the infrastructure crisis.

To the generations of Americans who helped build the United States into this great country, and particularly to my father, one hero in a greatest generation of heroes who served his country as a member of the Second Marine Corps Division in World War II. After his military service, he returned home to help build his country's infrastructure in water, wastewater, energy projects, and then highway projects during the Eisenhower administration. My father's commitment to God as a servant, his country as a soldier, and then as a Union tradesman helping to build this country's essential services, and his commitment to his family as a father made an immeasurable impact in my life.

Michael Underhill

About the Contributors

Henry Cisneros is chairman of CityView, a partner in building 40 communities in 12 states, incorporating more than 7000 homes with a home value of over $2 billion. After serving three terms as a city councilmember, in 1981, he became the first Hispanic American mayor of a major U.S. city, San Antonio, Texas. During his four terms as mayor, he helped rebuild the city's economic base and spurred the creation of jobs through massive infrastructure and downtown improvements, marking San Antonio as one of the nation's most progressive cities. After completing four terms as mayor, Henry formed Cisneros Asset Management Company, a fixed-income management firm. In 1992, President Clinton appointed him to be Secretary of the U.S. Department of Housing and Urban Development. In his role as the President's chief representative to the nation's cities, Henry personally worked in more than 200 U.S. cities in every one of the 50 states. After leaving HUD in 1997, he was president and chief operating officer of Univision Communications. He currently serves on Univision's board of directors. Henry has served as president of the National League of Cities, as deputy chair of the Federal Reserve Bank of Dallas, and as national chairman of the After-School All-Stars. He is currently a member of the advisory boards of the Bill and Melinda Gates Foundation and the Broad Foundation. In 2007, he was inducted into the National Association of Homebuilders (NAHB) "Builders Hall of Fame" and honored by the National Housing Conference as the "Housing Person of the Year." An author, editor, and/or collaborator on several books including *Interwoven Destinies: Cities and the Nation, Opportunity and Progress: A Bipartisan Platform for National Housing Policy*, and *Casa y Comunidad: Latino Home and Neighborhood Design*, Henry holds a BA and a MA in Urban and Regional Planning from Texas A&M University. He also earned an MA in Public Administration from Harvard University, studied urban economics at the Massachusetts Institute of Technology, holds a PhD in Public Administration from George Washington University, and has been awarded more than 20 honorary doctorates from leading universities. Henry served as an infantry officer in the U.S. Army. He is married to Mary Alice P. Cisneros, who in 2001 was elected to San Antonio's city council and they have three children—Teresa, Mercedes, and John Paul—and four grandchildren.

Peter Dickson is a technical director at Fortis Investments. He has 20 years of experience in engineering and heavy industry, 11 of them spent in the power sector, with a focus on renewable energy. Before joining Fortis Investments, Peter worked on renewable energy legislation with the United Nations Development Programme in Kazakhstan and prior to that, working for United Utilities and Hyder developing renewable energy projects in the United Kingdom. He is a chartered engineer and has a BA in Civil Engineering from the University of Glasgow.

Ian Savage Elliott was a research associate at Capital Innovations LLC responsible for conducting due diligence, analysis, and assessment on infrastructure investment opportunities, specializing in Energy and Natural Resources. Prior to Capital Innovations, Ian worked at Fletcher Asset Management, LLC focusing on quantitative analysis of asset allocation for both buy and sell side private equity transactions. Prior to Fletcher Asset Management, Ian worked with the Department of Homeland Security as a member of the Office of International Affairs. He earned a BA from Colgate University. Ian is currently pursuing higher education.

David N. Fleischer is a principal at Chickasaw Capital Management, LLC. He most recently was a managing director at Kayne Anderson Capital Advisors, LP, serving as a portfolio manager for their alternative investment fund and closed-end fund assets, which exceeded $1 billion. David was a managing director at Goldman Sachs & Co., serving on its investment policy and stock selection committees for over 10 years and was the business unit leader for the firm's energy research. He was responsible for investment research of MLPs, natural gas companies and gas utilities, and was an *Institutional Investor* ranked analyst for 16 consecutive years in natural gas. He graduated from the University of Pennsylvania with a BA in Economics in 1970. He received an MBA from The Wharton School of the University of Pennsylvania in 1976, and served four years active duty in the U.S. Navy, attaining the rank of Lieutenant Commander. He is a Chartered Financial Analyst.

Brian Foerster is a capital markets analyst and senior financial writer at Invesco. He joined Invesco in October 2007, and has 14 years of asset management industry experience. He is responsible for capital markets research and has authored and published numerous articles, white papers, and research reports used by clients, institutional consultants and the financial press. He has written extensively on infrastructure investing, emerging market debt, evolving theory and practice in asset allocation, and the liberalization of China's financial markets. Prior to joining Invesco, Brian worked for five years at ING Investment Management as an assistant vice president where he managed financial market research and client publications. He previously also worked at Fidelity Investments and New York Life as an investment analyst, focusing on quantitative research. Brian graduated from Boston College with degrees in Economics and English, and he is a Level II candidate in the CFA program. He also completed graduate coursework in economics and econometrics at Harvard University.

Stephan Forstmann has been a managing director at Duff and Phelps' New York office since 2005 and part of the firm's corporate finance consulting practice, focusing on portfolio valuations. He has more than 14 years of valuation and corporate finance experience. Prior to joining Duff & Phelps, he was an investment manager with Affentranger Associates, a private equity and corporate finance firm. He was also with the wealth management firm of Lombard Odier Darier Hentsch. As managing director, Stephan advises clients in the valuation of business enterprises, equity and debt interests, and transactional analysis. He has served a broad range of industries in recent years, focusing on alternative investments, and his clients have included various well-known alternative investment managers. He holds a PhD in business administration and an MBA from the University of St. Gallen in Switzerland. He is a certified public accountant.

Daniel F. Huang is a director at Duff & Phelps with over 20 years of professional experience advising a broad array of companies, ranging from specialized startup situations to multinational corporations. He currently provides valuation advisory services to a diverse spectrum of infrastructure, private equity, and other alternative investment firms. He has worked closely with a wide range of investment sponsors and strategies, including infrastructure, real estate, LBOs, venture capital, emerging markets, hedge funds, and specialized situations. He has originated and structured numerous investment opportunities and has been involved in all aspects of investment evaluation and due diligence. Daniel's experience also includes the valuation of business enterprises, equity and debt interests, transactional analysis as well as broad M&A advisory. Daniel has been actively involved in raising capital from public and private pension funds, banks, insurance companies, financial institutions, foundations, endowments, consultants, and financial advisors in North America, Europe, and Asia. Prior to Duff & Phelps, he was involved in sourcing and arranging institutional capital for a $4 billion infrastructure fund, which included a diversified portfolio of toll roads, marine container terminals, and electric and water utilities. He has also been involved in exploring Greenfield and Brownfield opportunities with prospective investors for public-private partnerships and privately negotiated infrastructure opportunities. He has been actively involved in capital-raising engagements encompassing in excess of $10 billion and has advised on structuring alternative investments across a variety of sectors, strategies, and geographies. He earned his MBA from The Wharton School, University of Pennsylvania, in finance and entrepreneurial management.

James L. Johnstone is a vice president at Chickasaw Capital Management, LLC, focused on institutional sales. Prior to Chickasaw Capital Management, he was vice president of institutional marketing for Janus Capital Group. Jim's expertise includes all facets of relationships with qualified retirement plans, foundations, endowments, high-net-worth individuals, and Taft-Hartley plans. He has over 16 years of senior level sales experience within the institutional asset management industry including tenures at PIMCO and Fidelity Investments. He graduated with a BS in economics from Florida State University in 1987.

David Kerr is a senior vice president at the Government of Singapore, Special Investments. David has more than 20 years' experience in infrastructure development and finance, including investment acquisition, management and divestment on behalf of principal investors. Previously, he held various positions at Deutsche Bank and Bechtel Enterprises Inc., the infrastructure finance and development arm of Bechtel Group Inc. David's experience includes key roles in airports, water/wastewater utilities, roads and energy transactions. He also previously worked for John Laing and Taylor Woodrow International where he participated in the development of large infrastructure projects around the world. David is a chartered engineer and a member of the Institution of Civil Engineers. He has served as president of the board of Lima Airport Partners, chairman of the board of Curacao Airport Partners and as a director of London Luton Airport. David has an MBA in finance from The Wharton School of the University of Pennsylvania, and graduated from the University of Strathclyde, Glasgow, with an honors degree in civil engineering.

Douglas W. Kimmelman is senior partner and founder of Energy Capital Partners, a private equity firm formed in 2005 to focus on investments in North American power generation, electric transmission, and midstream gas assets. The firm's first fund, Energy Capital Partners I, having completed a $2.25 billion fundraise, has invested in 13 entities in its core areas of focus. Highlights include the acquisition in 2006 of 15 predominately hydropower facilities from Northeast Utilities for $1.34 billion and their sale two years later to GDF Suez for approximately $2 billion; the construction of an $800 million gas-fired generation station in upstate New York coming on line in 2010; a 500-mile electric transmission new build project and the construction of the largest activated carbon production facility in the United States (mercury control for power plants). Prior to the formation of Energy Capital, Douglas was a partner of Goldman Sachs, having spent 22 years with the firm exclusively focused on electric and gas utility matters. He was instrumental in the formation of Goldman Sachs' principal investing activities in the power sector, helping to found Orion Power as well as helping to lead Goldman's investment program to add power assets at the corporate level. Collectively, these programs have resulted in the ownership of over 150 power units representing over $15 billion in investment capital. Douglas chairs the boards of both the Far Hills Country Day School and Crime Stoppers of Somerset County and is also the board president of The Willie Randolph Foundation. He resides in Bernardsville, New Jersey with his wife and four children. He received a BA in economics from Stanford University in 1982 and an MBA from the Wharton School of the University of Pennsylvania in 1984.

Scott Lawrence is an investment director at Fortis Investments. He has nine years of investment and operational experience in the renewable energy and commercial real estate sectors. Prior to joining Fortis Investments, Scott founded a development company that raised private equity finance for the development and construction of solar power plants in Spain. He started his career at Babson Capital Management underwriting commercial real estate debt. Scott holds an MBA from London Business School and a BSc from Cornell University.

Matthew G. Mead is a principal at Chickasaw Capital Management, LLC. He serves as a senior relationship manager, managing significant assets for clients of Chickasaw Capital. He started his investment management career with Goldman Sachs & Co.'s private wealth management group in Memphis, where he served for nine years and was a vice president. Matt advises families with substantial wealth, specializing in equity portfolio management, income equity management, fixed-income portfolio management, and single stock risk management. Matt received his BS from Birmingham-Southern College in 1990, double majoring in economics and finance. He received an MBA from the Fuqua School of Business, Duke University in 1992.

Wilbur L. Ross, Jr., is chairman and CEO of WL Ross & Co., LLC. One of the best-known turnaround financiers in the United States, having been involved in the restructuring of over $200 billion of defaulted companies' assets around the world, Wilbur was coined "the King of Bankruptcy" in

1988 by *Fortune* magazine. He organized International Steel Group (ISG) in April 2002 and was its board chairman. By acquiring Bethlehem and other troubled companies, ISG became the largest integrated steel company in North America. It was listed on the New York Stock Exchange until it merged with Mittal Steel to form the largest steel company in the world. Wilbur remains a director of ArcelorMittal. In October 2005, the firm teamed up with India's Housing Development Finance Corporation Limited, India's $9.5 billion mortgage finance institution, to invest in Indian corporate restructurings and turnarounds. In March 2004, the firm organized International Textile Group (ITG) by buying and consolidating two bankrupt companies, Burlington Industries and Cone Mills. On October 1, 2004, WL Ross organized International Coal Group to acquire out of bankruptcy Horizon Natural Resources and two other coal companies and went public, and in 2005, WL Ross formed International Automotive Components (IAC) to acquire Collins & Aikman's European operations and Lear's European interior plastics division. More recently, the firm acquired control of PLASCAR, the leading Brazilian automotive plastics company, Mitsubishi in Japan, Lear Corporation's U.S., European, and Asian interior plastics businesses, and certain North American plants of Collins & Aikman. IAC now has revenues of $5.5 billion and 23,000 employees in 17 countries. In 1999, President Kim Dae Jung awarded Wilbur a medal for his help during Korea's 1998 financial crisis. He is a former chairman of the Smithsonian National Board. Earlier, President Clinton had appointed him to the board of the U.S.-Russia Investment Fund, and he served as privatization advisor to former Mayor Rudolph Giuliani. Wilbur serves on the executive committee of the New York City Partnership and of the Japan Society and is a member of the Chairman's Circle of the U.S.-India Business Council. He is a member of the Business Roundtable and is a board member of the Yale University School of Management, which has presented him with its Legend of Leadership Award. He is also a member of the Committee on Capital Markets Regulation. China Institute presented him with its 2007 Blue Cloud Award. Wilbur holds a BA from Yale University and an MBA, with Distinction, from Harvard University.

Joseph Seliga is a partner in the Chicago office of the international law firm Mayer Brown, LLP. He is a member of Mayer Brown's Government and Global Trade Practice Group and Global Infrastructure practice. He practices in the area of state and local government law, representing public sector and private sector clients in a wide array of transactional, legislative, and regulatory matters. Joseph has extensive experience in large-scale government transactions, particularly in the infrastructure sector. He advised

the city of Chicago on the $1.83 billion concession and lease of the Chicago Skyway Toll Bridge from the early planning stages of the transaction through closing; the Indiana Finance Authority on the $3.8 billion concession and lease of the Indiana Toll Road; the city of Chicago on the $563 million concession and lease of the over 9000-space Chicago downtown underground parking garage system; the Northwest Parkway Public Highway Authority with respect to its $603 million concession and lease of the Northwest Parkway in Colorado; the Commonwealth of Pennsylvania related to the proposed $12.8 billion concession and lease of the Pennsylvania Turnpike; and the Port of Portland with respect to the proposed concession and lease of its Terminal 6 container facility. He also represented private sector bidders with respect to the Mid-Currituck Bridge project in North Carolina and the Jackson, Mississippi Airport Parkway project. Joseph is currently advising the city of Chicago with respect to the proposed privatization of Chicago Midway International Airport; the Port of the Americas Authority related to its planned concession for the operation of the Port of the Americas in Ponce, Puerto Rico; and CenterPoint Properties concerning its proposal to enter into a long-term public-private partnership related to the Port of Virginia. Joseph received his undergraduate degree magna cum laude from Georgetown University, an MA with Distinction from the University of Leicester, where he studied as a Marshall Scholar, and a JD cum laude from Northwestern University School of Law.

Zhongmin Shen is the chief executive officer of Huaneng Invesco WLR Investment Consulting Company Ltd., a joint venture of Huaneng, the leading Chinese power and energy conglomerate, and Invesco/WLRoss. Huaneng Invesco WLR is the principal advisor to WLR China Energy Infrastructure Fund, a China-focused private equity fund focusing on coal mining and coal-fired power, clean and renewable energy and other energy-related investments. Before joining Huaneng Invesco WLR, Zhongmin was a managing director at CLP Holdings Limited (China Light and Power, CLP), which is one of the largest investor-owned power businesses in Asia, listed in Hong Kong as a member of HSI Constituents. CLP is the largest external/foreign investor in the power industry in China with generating capacities in coal-fired, nuclear, hydro, wind, and biomass power. Prior to joining CLP, Zhongmin had over 12 years of experience in business development, energy project investment and financing, merger and acquisition, and joint venture management in the power and energy industry in China. From 2003 to 2006, Zhongmin was executive director and chief operating officer of China Resources Power Holdings Co., Ltd (CRP), which is listed in Hong Kong (a member of HSI Constituents) and majority owned by China Resources

Holdings Co., a major Chinese state-owned conglomerate. He was a key member of CRP's initial public offering process in 2003 and a core member of CRP's management team that made the company the fastest growing and most profitable independent power producer operating in the power generating business in China. From 1997 to 2003, Zhongmin was with Sithe Energies, Inc., a New York-based independent power producer majority owned by Vivendi, and was managing director of Sithe China Holdings Limited. He started his power and energy career in 1994 with Wheelabrator Technologies, Inc., a New York-listed energy and environmental services company that was majority owned by Waste Management, Inc. Zhongmin received a BS in chemistry and an LLM from Beijing University, an MA in economics from the University of Tennessee, and an Executive MBA from the Guanghua School of Management of Beijing University.

Robert M.T. Walker is a research analyst at Chickasaw Capital Management, LLC. He started his investment management career with Haas, Incorporated, a family office in Memphis. He most recently was a research analyst with Trinity Capital, an equity hedge fund. Robert received his BA from Rhodes College in 1999, with a history major and a business administration minor. He received an MBA from the Owen Graduate School of Management, Vanderbilt University in 2005 where he was the chairman of the Max Adler Student Investment Fund.

Michael D. Underhill is the chief executive officer and chief investment officer of Capital Innovations LLC, a global infrastructure investment advisory firm established in 2007. He is responsible for managing the firm's investment activities and chairing the firm's investment committee. Michael is a frequently quoted expert on the infrastructure industry, and has served as a resource in Dow Jones Publications, *Investments Pensions Europe*, *The Economist*, *Pension and Investments*, and numerous industry journals. In addition, Michael has appeared on dozens of conference panels and speaking engagements as an infrastructure industry expert. Michael has directly advised some of the largest Sovereign Wealth Funds, Public Pension Funds and Financial Institutions on institutional investments into the infrastructure sector across unlisted and listed infrastructure securities. Prior to founding Capital Innovations LLC, Michael was a managing director at an $18 billion private investment firm where he was involved in the direct investment, co-investment, and asset management businesses. During the span of his career, he has been involved in over $15 billion of investment management transactions. He began his career 18 years ago with Lehman Brothers working on quantitative analysis of fixed-income securities. Michael earned a BS in economics from Pennsylvania State University. He has completed post-graduate coursework from Pepperdine University, Stanford Law School and participated in the Mercosur Economic studies at the Universidad Del Salvador. He is a member of the American Economics Association. He is active in raising money for cancer research and has completed 24 marathons in the spirit of fundraising and to promote cancer awareness.

Disclaimer

Capital Innovations LLC, Hartland, Wisconsin 53029, does not undertake to advise of changes in the information in chapters by its employees. Their materials have been prepared solely for informational purposes based on information generally available to the public from sources believed to be reliable. Capital Innovations makes no representation with respect to the accuracy or completeness of these materials, whose content may change without notice. Capital Innovations disclaims any and all liability relating to these materials, and makes no express or implied representations or warranties concerning the statements made in, or omissions from, these materials. No portion of this publication may be reproduced in any format or by any means including electronically or mechanically, by photocopying, recording or by any information storage or retrieval system, or by any other form or manner whatsoever, without the prior written consent of Capital Innovations.

Capital Innovations does not guarantee the accuracy and/or completeness of the S&P Global Infrastructure Index, any data included therein, or any data from which it is based, and Capital Innovations shall have no liability for any errors, omissions, or interruptions therein. Capital Innovations makes no warranty, expressed or implied, as to results to be obtained from the use of the S&P Global Infrastructure Index. Capital Innovations makes no expressed or implied warranties, and expressly disclaims all warranties of merchantability or fitness for a particular purpose or use with respect to the S&P Global Infrastructure Index or any data included therein. Without limiting any of the foregoing, in no event shall Capital Innovations have any liability for any special, punitive, indirect, or consequential damages (including lost profits), even if notified of the possibility of such damages.

Capital Innovations does not sponsor, endorse, sell, or promote any investment fund or other vehicle that is offered by third parties and that seeks to provide an investment return based on the returns of the S&P Global Infrastructure Index. A decision to invest in any such investment fund or other vehicle should not be made in reliance on any of the statements set forth in this document. Prospective investors are advised to make an investment in any such fund or vehicle only after carefully considering the risks associated with investing in such funds, as detailed in an offering memorandum or similar document that is prepared by or on behalf of the issuer of the investment fund or vehicle.

Analytic services and products provided by Capital Innovations are the result of separate activities designed to preserve the independence and objectivity of each analytic process. Capital Innovations has established policies and procedures to maintain the confidentiality of nonpublic information received during each analytic process.

The Handbook of Infrastructure Investing

CHAPTER 1

America's Essential Infrastructure

A Key to Competitiveness

Henry Cisneros
Chairman, CityView

W hen most Americans hear the increasingly frequent references to *infrastructure* they summon up only ill-defined images. Some call to mind the hulking gray mass of crumbling bridges and the disruption of leaking water lines; others associate it vaguely with public works jobs and federal stimulus funds; and still others are numbed to the point of disinterest by the bureaucratic jargon. In truth, infrastructure is at the core of one of the most urgent aspects of the United States' well-being: our national competitiveness. The U.S. competiveness determines whether the products our industries create are viable in world markets, whether our economy is strong enough to enhance national income and wealth, and whether our society can sustain a high quality of life.

National competiveness depends on continual improvements in productivity, the value of output we create per unit of resource devoted to its production, usually measured as gross domestic product (GDP) per capita or per job. There are many factors that contribute to steadily improving productivity. Among them are advances in technology and innovation, higher level skills and education, access to capital, vibrant entrepreneurship, and functioning rules for free markets. More and more economic scholars such as Professor Michael Porter of the Harvard Business School include the range of physical and communications support systems—modern infrastructure—as essential components of productivity. It may be helpful to think of infrastructure as the basic systems that bridge distance and bring productive

EXHIBIT 1.1 Types of Infrastructure

Transportation	Communication	Energy and Utilities	Social Infrastructure
Roads	Telephone systems	Electricity distribution and generation	Universities
Bridges	Cell towers	Gas storage and distribution	Schools
Tunnels	Cable networks	Water supply	Hospitals
Airports	WiFi	Wasterwater treatment	Sports stadiums
Rail systems	Satellite	Renewable energy	Community facilities
Seaports	Television		Public housing
Shipping	Radio		Prisons
Cargo	Other systems		Corrections centers
Logistical centers			
Urban mass transit			

inputs together; that bring materials, products, equipment, information, and people together; and that in fundamental ways bring all the critical factors of productivity to bear across time and space.

As Exhibit 1.1 demonstrates, infrastructure includes the systems of transportation that are used to move materials and industrial goods to fabrication and assembly points and then to distribute finished products to merchants and consumers. Similarly, the infrastructure of communications connects producers and purchasers in our economy as well as conveys marketing through advertising, broadcasts entertainment, and transmits personal messages. Infrastructure is also critical in providing the water and power needed for industrial, commercial, and residential purposes. The generation of electricity from coal, nuclear, natural gas, hydro, wind or solar sources and its distribution through the power grid are essential inputs to national production and secure human safety and comfort. The institutions that extend education, health care, civic engagement and jurisprudence, such as universities, schools, civic centers and public buildings of various kinds, constitute the public social infrastructure of the nation.

The realization that the nation's infrastructure is comprised of the assets that connect the productive capacities of the society and that mobilize the physical inputs to our economy is particularly important as we consider the way the modern U.S. economy actually functions. Infrastructure should be regarded as among the most basic and essential dimensions in the workings of U.S. society. Many societal interactions are based on ideas, abstractions, and symbolic or numerical representations. Many modern processes involve information flows, electronic pulses, higher order cognitive exchanges related to creative thought and quantitative analyses. But it is physical infrastructure that makes possible not only the movement of the materials and products that are quantified in those digital messages but it also makes possible the electronic pulses themselves.

Even the most modern of companies, including those regarded as Information Era breakthroughs such as Amazon.com, rely intensely on efficient and reliable physical infrastructure. Clearly, the communications by which a consumer shops on Amazon.com via the Internet relies on channels of high-speed electronic distribution lines as well as the capacities of massive server facilities in physical locations across the country. Then the consumer goods, which have been ordered via Amazon.com and were manufactured in fabrication plants and stored in warehouses utilizing sophisticated logistical technologies, are rapidly shipped through a network of cargo aircraft and overland trucks with the goal of having products to the consumer within a day or at most several days. Amazon is an example of the interface between the information economy and the physical economy of materials and products that relies so heavily on state-of-the-art infrastructure.

This chapter describes in a new way three building-blocks of U.S. competitiveness and the core role of infrastructure in each case. The three are: the global economy's increasing dependence on modern logistics; the power of industry clusters primed to act as linked units of economic competiveness; and the role of metropolitan areas as engines of prosperity for the nation. A fourth building-block is the overarching combination of national population growth, the demand for built space that it will drive and the role of innovation in infrastructure development.

OUR ECONOMY IS INCREASINGLY DEPENDENT ON MODERN LOGISTICS

The U.S. economy has evolved into complex synapses of national and global transactions. Coal mined in Wyoming is essential to the operation of technology firms in Houston; computer software engineered in Silicon Valley is matched with computer hardware manufactured in North Carolina; and materials imported from Indonesia are transferred from ships onto trucks at the Port of Long Beach en route to assembly warehouses in Riverside, California, before being loaded onto rail cars for shipment to big box stores in Kansas City. These kinds of transactions are occurring every moment of every day across the United States and are highly dependent on durable infrastructure. When the infrastructure proves inadequate to the task, the U.S. economy suffers. In his work on U.S. competitiveness, Professor Michael

Porter of Harvard has singled out the factors that have "hobbled America's entrepreneurial strength by needlessly driving up the cost and complexity of doing business."[1] Specifically, he writes: "Infrastructure bottlenecks, due to neglect and poorly directed spending, are driving up costs in an economy increasingly dependent on logistics."

International Trade

One area of the U.S. economy where the infrastructure of logistics must flow efficiently is international trade and foreign investment. Global trade has become an increasingly important dimension of the U.S. economy. Imports to and exports from the United States now represent 25 percent of GDP up from 6 percent in 1950.[2] That robust volume of international trade depends heavily on logistical movement of goods by ship into ports, by rail and truck overland, and by air cargo.

Port authorities on both coasts have invested in port infrastructure that is among the best in the world. Los Angeles/Long Beach, Seattle, San Francisco/Oakland, New York/New Jersey, the Chesapeake region, Miami, and Houston—all have made massive investments in the capacity to off-load shipping containers and to transfer them to barges, trains, and trucks. Because so many imports into the United States arrive from Asia, a heavy volume of the container traffic into the United States enters at the Ports of Long Beach and Los Angeles. Those ports handled 15.7 million units of containers in 2007. The Ports of New York/New Jersey handled 5.3 million containers; Seattle/Tacoma, 3.9 million; Savannah, Georgia, 2.9 million; and Oakland, 2.6 million according to the American Association of Port Authorities.[3]

Though the containers arrive at these coastal ports, the products must be moved to warehouses, retail stores, and consumers across the country. Moving cargo by rail from ports has become a dominant channel for moving goods to large distribution centers in the heartland of the nation. There, containers can be off-loaded from trains and moved by trucks to warehouses where goods can be sorted, assembled, and prepared for wholesale and retail sales. Large-scale "inland ports" have been created in cities such as Chicago, Dallas, Kansas City, and Indianapolis. They employ the most modern inter-modal technologies to classify merchandise, to package and label products, and to prepare them for marketing.

Rapid Transport of High-Value Goods

The modern economy also places a premium on the rapid movement of certain products. Smaller, higher value and time-sensitive products are flown directly into air cargo hubs such as those in Memphis via Fed Ex, Louisville with UPS, or to Dallas and Chicago by other carriers. Alliance Airport in Dallas is an example of an air hub built specifically for the handling of cargo. Despite the existence of one the largest and most efficient airports in the country at Dallas/Ft. Worth International, the designers of Alliance Airport recognized the need for a facility in the center of the United States devoted strictly to cargo and equipped with the latest technologies for handling high value freight. Alliance is now home to more than 200 companies utilizing 29 million square feet of processing facilities and includes an intermodal facility that handles more than 600,000 cargo enplanements per year.[4]

Global Communications

Dependence on instantaneous worldwide communications is another important dimension of the interface between the workings of the modern global economy and infrastructure. A report by the Chicago Council on Global Affairs that presented recommendations to guide Chicago's participation in the global economy included the following observation: "Ubiquitous high-bandwidth Internet connectivity is essential for any city to flourish in a global environment. Businesses must be visible on the Web and be able to engage in E-commerce."[5] The Chicago report makes reference to an analysis commissioned by the Communications Workers of America that documents that Internet speed in Japan is 61 megabits per second or more than 30 times faster than the U.S. broadband speed of 1.97 megabits per second. Other countries that have higher broadband speed than the United States include South Korea at 45 megabits, France at 17 megabits, and Canada at 7 megabits.

While breakthroughs in the speed of transmission and breadth of content of digital communications over the last decades—particularly the widespread expansion of wireless communications—are breathtaking, it cannot be taken for granted the degree to which the hard infrastructure of transmission towers, satellites, power generators, and antennae farms make the convergence of large volumes of voice, data, and graphic communications possible. Tangible evidence of the infrastructure of instantaneous electronic communications are the massive data centers that are increasingly becoming the nerve centers of the economy and of society. Data centers are critical points of convergence in the generation of ever faster and more robust data transmission, striving to produce more computing power per square foot for the lowest possible expenditure in resources. The technology of computing infrastructure that makes it possible for a Google search to be executed in .15 seconds is financed in large measure by the private sector. But what is easy to miss is the dependence by data centers on the public power capabilities of the locations in which they are set. Centers such as the 700,000-square-foot facilities built by Microsoft are "a sprawling array of servers, local balancers, routers, fire walls, tape-backup libraries, and database machines, all resting on a raised floor of removable white tiles, beneath which run neatly arrayed bundles of power cabling."[6] And the huge electrical flows required to power the data centers are equaled by the amount of electricity required to cool them. Local utilities are building energy capability in order to prepare for the expectation of more data centers in their service areas. San Antonio, Texas, for example is the site of a Microsoft data center and is now planning future energy capacity in order to support more technology industries. It proposes diversifying its municipally owned power generation from the present base of coal, natural gas, and oil by adding wind and additional nuclear capability. Data centers are an example of the dependence of communications and information technologies on basic infrastructure because the cost of power is so important and interruptions of power are so damaging. Metropolitan areas that have adequate power reserves will have a major advantage in economic development.

The fields of logistics, supply chain management, transportation and global communications are increasingly critical to the functioning of the national economy. Some experts believe that the availability of state-of-the-art logistical capability, supported by massive infrastructure investment, will determine economic development opportunities in the new century. Arnold Perl, Chair of the Memphis Logistics Council, states: "Access is to the 21st century what location was to the 20th."[7] Access to materials, industrial processes, information, electrical power and markets will determine the competitiveness of industries, regions, and nations. Dependence on modern infrastructure could not be clearer.

SUCCESSFUL INDUSTRY LINKAGES CREATE STRONG ECONOMIC CLUSTERS

Michael Porter describes the U.S. economy as composed of thousands of clusters of firms geographically concentrated into poles of sectoral strength across the nation.[8] Linkages between firms and industries create clusters that become the actual platforms for global transactions and are the geographic hot-houses of U.S. productivity. Clusters tend to form bottom-up in different regions of the nation and are characterized by many individual business decisions and investments. Successful clusters of firms, functioning as parts of global chains of companies and developing the knowledge and skills needed to enhance business prowess, define the prospects of regions. This is equally true for manufacturing firms and for enterprises in advanced services. Principal firms are joined by supplier firms, each making individual investments in the technologies required to participate in the industry cluster. An industry cluster at first forms around infrastructure suited to its specific industries and in time creates the need for more extensive and more advanced infrastructure. By definition, a cluster of industries relies on linkages, such as efficient routes for the movement of raw materials and parts for assembly, cost-effective instantaneous communications, common demands for water or power, or shared manpower needs. These linkages, figuratively the bones and the connecting cartilage and tendons of the cluster, constitute the infrastructure it needs to function and to grow.

Infrastructure Creates Cluster Linkages

An example of how infrastructure links an industry cluster is the supplier concentration that includes 21 automotive supply firms surrounding the Toyota plant in San Antonio. Toyota built a facility capable of producing 200,000 Tundra pick-up trucks and provided space within the footprint of the plant site for supplier firms who wished to locate there. Twenty-one firms have built fabrication and assembly plants on site and avail themselves of the shared rail and truck facilities that serve the complex. The extension of rail lines to the site required public intervention in order to assure that both the Burlington Northern Railroad and the Union Pacific Railroad could ship to the plants. Once the necessary accords were reached and the rail lines built, a cluster of automotive firms formed which now extends to support plants in South Texas and Northern Mexico.

Another example of how transportation infrastructure creates linkages for businesses is the UPS Worldport sorting system at Louisville International Airport. It is a 4 million square foot facility presently being expanded by an additional 1.2 million square feet. Its access to 250 daily flights and to parking facilities for 117 cargo jets has attracted a cluster of firms that rely on transportation solutions.[9] UPS has perfected what it calls "end-of-runway service," to describe the access available to firms that locate in proximity to Worldport in order to be able to fill online orders and ship immediately. Firms are able to take orders and have them in consumers' hands the next day anywhere in the United States because they can insert products into the UPS system within hours. Access to UPS's distribution network has created a cluster of shipping-sensitive firms which include Stride Rite, Johnson & Johnson, Ann Taylor, Zappos, and over 110 other companies.

Transportation infrastructure has also attracted major companies to Memphis. An April 2009 report in *Urban Land* states the following: "Memphis is known as a 'quadrimodal' city. It includes the largest cargo airport in the world, the third-largest rail center (behind Chicago and St. Louis), and the second-largest water port on the Mississippi River, and it is within range of more cities by overnight truck (600 miles) than any other U.S. city."[10] Memphis has evolved as an inland port serving the entire nation from a central location. The *Urban Land* report continues: "Major companies with headquarters or significant space in Memphis include AutoZone, Williams-Sonoma (more than 5 million square feet), DDN (pharmaceutical logistics), Cummings Diesel, Nissan, Kyocera, Nike, and Technicolor."

The science of analyzing industrial clusters as engines for the American economy is creating greater understanding of both the functioning of clusters and the infrastructure linkages that make them possible. The established clusters across the United States—including the biosciences cluster in the Washington/Baltimore area, telecommunications in Dallas, computer software development in Silicon Valley, biotechnology in the Research Triangle of North Carolina, automotive research and engineering in Michigan, aircraft manufacturing in Seattle, new media in Los Angeles, and finance in New York—are built on historical antecedents, are financed by specialized investment firms, involve specialized legal and accounting capabilities, and are supported by targeted educational and training programs. Each is also served by infrastructure essential to its function, by air routes, road and highway access, specialized communications, water supplies, electrical distribution, and various kinds of public works. When successful, the interwoven character and mutual uplift of firms in multiple industry clusters can grow into economic rationale strong enough to drive another building-block of national competitiveness, the economic engines which are the United States' major metropolitan areas.

STRENGTHENING COMPETITIVE METROPOLITAN ECONOMIES

The Brookings Institution has produced extensive research that describes the role of metropolitan areas in the U.S. economy. While 65 percent of Americans live in just the 100 largest metropolitan areas, more than 75 percent of GDP, 76 percent of knowledge jobs, 78 percent of patent activity, 81 percent of research and development (R&D) employment, and 94 percent of venture capital funding are generated in those metropolitan areas.[11] A report of the Brookings Metropolitan Policy Center states:

> *Today, our nation—and our economy—is metropolitan. U.S. metropolitan areas—complex regions of interwoven cities and suburbs—are home to more than eight in ten Americans and jobs. . . . They concentrate and strengthen the assets that drive our economic*

productivity, grow the skills and incomes of our workers, and contribute to our environmental sustainability. Our major metro areas reflect the face of the U.S. in a global economy where, for the first time, more than half of the world's population is metropolitan.

The major forces that contribute to national competiveness play out in a decentralized pattern in metropolitan areas across the nation: the presence of strong industry clusters, the availability of highly skilled talent, the capacities of entrepreneurs and investors, the existence of constructive regulatory structures, and the strength of regional infrastructure. Porter observes:

The federal government has also failed to recognize and support the decentralization and regional specialization that drive our economy. Washington still acts as if the federal level is where the action is. Beltway bureaucrats spend many billions of dollars on top-down, highly fragmented federal economic development programs. Yet these programs are not designed to support regional clusters nor do they send money where it will have the greatest impact in each region.[12]

National economic strategy must encompass the pragmatic determinants of competitiveness and productivity, which percolate up from the metropolitan institutions where human capital is developed, where on-the-ground environmental challenges are resolved, where investment decisions are made, where states and localities legislate regulatory frameworks, and where the next generation of infrastructure must be built.

Metro Economies Need Basic Infrastructure

Like electrical power, water is a basic resource that supports the new economy. Assuring a future water supply for a metropolitan area is one of the most critical imperatives of regional leadership. In water-scarce areas of the western United States, metropolitan strategies to acquire water resources or to conserve water determine growth prospects. Water is a critical resource for industrial processes, for consumer use, for recreational uses, for public amenities, and plays a critical role in business decisions. Metros such as Phoenix have developed compacts for the development of water resources, such as the Central Arizona Project that provides access to water from the Colorado River in order to meet the needs of consumers and industries. The long history of water conflicts between Northern and Southern California's metropolitan areas underscores its significance as basic infrastructure.

Basic transportation infrastructure is central to the historic role of hub metros such as Chicago, the nation's leading rail center and the only city in the country where all six Class One North American railroads intersect.[13] Every day 500 freight trains hauling 37,500 rail cars travel through Chicago. That daily number is expected to grow to 67,000 train cars by 2020, requiring a commitment to expanded rail infrastructure. More containers are transferred in Chicago from train to truck than in another city in the Western Hemisphere and Chicago is the fifth largest intermodal container handler in the world. Intermodal shipments grew by 8 percent in 2006 as increasing imports from Asia are transported to the U.S. heartland. But railroads now must allow more than 30 hours to move rail freight across the city; as a result, many shipments spend more time getting across Chicago then they do in transit from the coasts to Chicago. Metropolitan infrastructure improvements to reduce that congestion would serve not only the economy of the region but of the Midwest and of the nation.

Chicago's role as the transportation hub of the Midwest also depends on expedited passenger traffic through O'Hare International Airport. The report of the Chicago Council on Global Affairs states:

> *As global commerce grows so does global travel. That means that a city with the most international non-stop links is the city most connected to the globe. A city that stands at the center of the global aviation system is like a town on a major highway—it is the place that gets the business.*[14]

The report calls for a $6.6 billion modernization program for O'Hare Airport which, along with the airports serving metropolitan Atlanta, Los Angeles, Dallas/Ft. Worth, and Denver, was among the 10 busiest airports in the world in 2007.

The Future Infrastructure of Metros

The new economy will also require public investment beyond traditional infrastructure. Investment in higher education and worker training will involve not just the physical construction of schools, community colleges, and universities, but investment in technology to extend curricula and broaden access to rigorous skills development. The iron-clad equations of the new U.S. economy are: "High skills = high wages; low skills = low wages." The nation's hopes for a broader middle class require investment in the technology infrastructure of human capital development.

The actual workings of metropolitan areas as engines of the national economy can involve several metropolitan areas in a cohesive network. The

Texas Triangle has Dallas, Houston, and San Antonio as its corners; but within the Triangle are such important university and research centers as Austin and the University of Texas and College Station and Texas A&M University. The highway network that connects this complex of metro areas needs expansion to ensure the rapid movement of goods and people across the region. The IH-35 spine that links San Antonio, Austin, and Dallas-Ft. Worth is known as the NAFTA Corridor because of the volume of cargo it carries from Mexico into the central United States. Texas is now building toll roads as parallel routes in order to allow truck traffic to bypass the congestion on the 60-year-old IH-35 roadway. Planning is accelerating to add rail connections that would allow the Texas Triangle to be connected in the manner of major metropolitan centers in Europe and Japan.

A similar nexus of metropolitan synergy that exists is the Washington-Baltimore complex. The region is home to the most important governmental center in the world, but it also sustains numerous business, research, educational, and biomedical job generators. Mobility is served by road, tunnel, and rail facilities; but the region is linked to the nation and the world by three airports—Reagan National in Washington, Dulles in Virginia, and Baltimore-Washington International in Baltimore—each scheduled for continuous expansion.

POPULATION GROWTH, BUILDING NEEDS, AND INNOVATION IN INFRASTRUCTURE

Among the other major forces that will shape national competiveness and well-being are the growth of national population and its effects on U.S. markets. The nation's population will grow from approximately 306 million people in 2009 to about 395 million by 2050, an increase of about 90 million people in the next 40 years. As evident in Exhibit 1.2, the United States, which is the third most populous nation in the world today behind China and India, will remain the third most populous country in 2050, while the Russian Federation and Japan will decline in population rank among the nations of the world and perhaps even in absolute population.[15]

Exhibit 1.3 describes population changes between 2005 and 2050 among the northern industrial nations and projects population declines in Spain, Germany, Italy, and Japan. Russell Shorto described in the *New York Times* how social scientists Hans-Peter Kohler, Jose Antonio Ortega, and Francesco Billari in a 2002 study found that birthrates in some European nations have dipped below 1.3 percent, the rate at which a country's population would decline by half within 45 years. In the mid 1960s, Europe was 12.5 percent of world population; it is 7.2 percent today and by 2050

EXHIBIT 1.2   Most Populous Countries 2005 and 2050

Country	2005 Population	Rank	Country	2050 Population	Rank
China	1316	1	India	1593	1
India	1103	2	China	1392	2
USA	298	3	USA	395	3
Indonesia	223	4	Pakistan	305	4
Brazil	186	5	Indonesia	285	5
Pakistan	158	6	Nigeria	258	6
Russian Federation	143	7	Brazil	253	7
Bangladesh	142	8	Bangladesh	243	8
Nigeria	132	9	Democratic Republic of Congo	177	9
Japan	128	10	Ethiopia	170	10

Note: Numbers are in millions.
Source: United Nations Population Division.

will drop to 5 percent. Mark Steyn, author of *America Alone: The End of the World as We Know It*, states: "These countries are going out of business."[16]

The United States by contrast will grow, in large part due to the growth of minority populations already within the country, as well as immigrants who will arrive here in the years to come. Minority families tend to be younger than the national average and are larger than average, creating a population trajectory that ensures that the United States will continue to grow in population as well as in markets. The reality of steady population growth and estimates of annual GDP growth of about 3 percent, as shown in Exhibit 1.4, will drive the need for continued development of the physical facilities to support that growth. The growth of population and consumer markets will create a need for new residences, for expanded plants to grow current product lines and for new facilities to provide products and services not yet developed.

Meeting the Need for Built Space

The Brookings Institution has projected levels of demand for expansion of the built environment in the United States. A Brookings study prepared by Professor Arthur Nelson of Virginia Tech estimates that there were 296 billion square feet of built structures in the United States in the year 2000.[17]

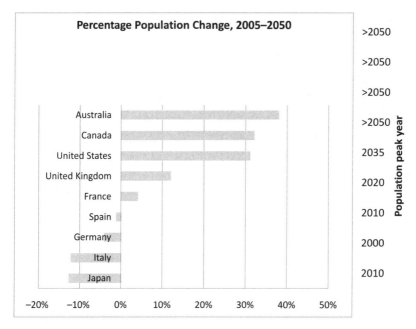

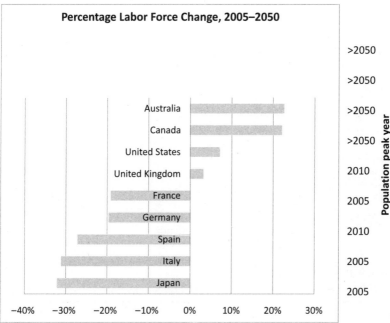

EXHIBIT 1.3 Population and labor force change in selected mature economies (percent), 2005–2050

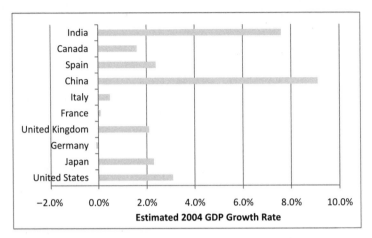

EXHIBIT 1.4 World's top 10 economic countries, 2004

As Exhibit 1.5 describes, by 2030 the nation will need 426 billion square feet of space for residential, commercial, and industrial purposes. That is an increase of 131 billion square feet, which when added to the 82 billion square feet of estimated replacement needs, means that the nation must build more than 213 billion square feet of additional space. That is about two-thirds the volume of the existing built stock in the U.S., a massive amount of construction.

EXHIBIT 1.5 Summary of U.S. Built Space: Existing and Needed, 2005 and 2030

	2000	Needed to Be Built	2005	2030
Total built space[a]	295.9	New:	131.4	426.3
		Replacement:	82.0	
		Total:	13.4	
Residential units[b]	115.9	New:	38.8	154.8
		Replacement:	20.1	
Residential units[a]	176.7	New and Replacement:	108.7	254.7
Commercial and institutional space[a]	106.7	New and Replacement:	96.4	159.3
Industrial facilities[a]	12.3	New and Replacement:	8.2	13.2

Notes:
[a]in billions of square feet
[b]in millions of units

Professor Nelson's calculation for total building needs is equally impressive in its component parts. The nation, for example, had 116 million housing units in the year 2000. It is estimated by 2030 that 59 million additional units will be needed, including 39 million for growth and 20 million to replace aged or deteriorated stock. By that calculation, a volume of housing units roughly equivalent to 50 percent of the nation's existing housing stock will have to be built over the first half of the 21st century.

The Brookings report estimates that the nation has about 107 million square feet of commercial and institutional space that must grow to 159 million square feet by 2030, a total of 96 million square feet to be constructed new and for replacement. That figure represents about 90 percent of the square footage in existence in 2000. With respect to industrial facilities, the Brookings report estimates that there were 12.3 million square feet in existence 2000 which must grow by 8.2 million square feet of new and replacement facilities by 2030, representing about 67 percent of the total in existence in 2000. By any account, such a scale of projected physical structures to be built is immense and underscores not only the growth challenges before the country but the infrastructure challenges as well. The very act of constructing that amount of built space will require additional transportation, water, power, communications, and social infrastructure. To the challenge of building infrastructure to support such growth must be added the replacement of today's aging and obsolete infrastructure as well as the emplacement of new generations of infrastructure yet to be developed in the communications, energy, and transportation arenas.

Next Infrastructure

Some of the infrastructure to be constructed will incorporate new technologies and assume new forms and functions. One of the most likely areas of infrastructure progress is alternative energy. In the short run, alternative energy innovation means modernizing the electric grid, investing in large-scale public transit, incorporation of smart technologies in homes and buildings, and investment in more efficient automobiles and roadway systems.[18] Developments in renewable energy—including wind, solar, and biomass power—are being funded by traditional financial sources, as electrical utilities replace traditional power generation with renewable energy technologies. The American Public Power Association and the Large Public Power Council have undertaken a joint initiative to promote energy efficiency and clean energy by publicly owned utilities.[19] In Arizona, the world's largest solar plant, capable of generating 280 megawatts, is now under construction and in California, Pacific Gas and Electric and Southern California Edison are embarking on massive solar energy projects. X-Cel Energy is building the nation's first "Smart-Grid" city installing more than 15,000 advanced residential meters in Boulder and more than 100 miles of cable over power lines for broadband transmission.

State-level public investments in energy infrastructure are also underway, such as Michigan's investment in a clean energy transmission network that would bring wind power from the Dakotas, Iowa, and Minnesota to population centers in the Midwest. The plan calls for 3,000 miles of power lines and would cost $12 billion. Maine is already New England's largest wind energy producer and has plans to produce an additional 503 megawatts from wind power over the next few years. And the State of New Jersey inaugurated the Atlantic City Convention Center's Solar System, which makes it the largest single-roof solar panel in the nation.

Parallel innovations in every dimension of infrastructure development and of infrastructure finance suggest that the field is poised for major breakthroughs. The challenges of sustaining the United States' competitiveness requires heightened levels of innovation, investment, and public and private sector commitment to the next generation of infrastructure.

CONCLUSION

The United States faces challenges in a world that is rapidly changing. The most basic facets of national well-being—international security, domestic prosperity, measures of quality of life, the values of inclusion and opportunity—depend on sustaining competitiveness and productivity in the United States. This chapter has attempted to make a straightforward case: that as the global economy has evolved, critical new building-blocks of national competitiveness have emerged. Modern logistics must be able to move the contents of global production rapidly and continuously to points of convergence. That effective confluence of inputs enables mutually supportive clusters of firms to compete globally and to create jobs. When multiple clusters grow to scale, metropolitan areas become strong enough to be vibrant platforms for national prosperity. And propelling these progressions are continuous fuel injections of population growth, of building needs, and of innovation.

In this context, infrastructure must be understood as the assets and systems that enable these building-blocks to be arrayed together. Americans must move beyond thinking of our infrastructure challenge as only replacing the massive hulks of 19th century public works. The nation must imagine infrastructure that is not just more of the same, just expanded for greater capacity. Our public and private leaders must commit to infrastructure that is new not only in the date of its construction, but is new in the creativity of how it applies new technologies, how it gets more for less, how it protects the environment, and how it advances national competitiveness. At stake is nothing less than the well-being of the American people.

ENDNOTES

1. Michael E. Porter, "Why America Needs an Economic Strategy," *BusinessWeek*, November 10, 2008, 41.
2. Sam Newberg, "Logistical Demand," *Urban Land*, April, 2009, 61.
3. Id., 62.
4. Id., 63.
5. *The Global Edge: An Agenda for Chicago's Future*, The Chicago Council on Global Affairs, 2007, 35–36.
6. Tom Vanderbilt, "Datatecture," *New York Times Sunday Magazine*, June 14, 2009, 32.
7. Arnold Perl, as quoted in Newberg, 65.
8. Michael E. Porter, Address at Brookings Metropolitan Policy Program Summit, Washington, DC, June 12, 2008.
9. Newberg, 64.
10. Id., 65.
11. *Metro Nation: How U.S. Metropolitan Areas Fund American Prosperity*, Metropolitan Policy Program, The Brookings Institution, 2007, 7.
12. Michael E. Porter, "Why America Needs an Economic Strategy," 41.
13. *The Global Edge*, 24.
14. Id., 33–34.
15. M. Leanne Lachman, *Global Demographics and Their Real Estate Investment Implications*, The Urban Land Institute, 2006, 2, 5.
16. Russell Shorto, "No Hay Bebes? Keine Kinder," *New York Times Sunday Magazine*, June 29, 2008, 36–37.
17. Arthur C. Nelson, "Toward a New Metropolis: The Opportunity to Rebuild America." A discussion paper prepared for The Brookings Institution Metropolitan Policy Program, December 2004.
18. Frances Beinecke, "Clean Energy: The Next Economic Engine," *Poder Enterprise Magazine*, May, 2009, 44.
19. Elise Morales, "Going Green Moves into the Mainstream," *Poder Enterprise Magazine*, May 2009, 46–47.

CHAPTER 2

Transportation Infrastructure

David Kerr
GIC Special Investments

INTRODUCTION

Transportation-related infrastructure—roads, bridges, tunnels, railways, canals, seaports, and airports—is such a fundamental cornerstone of the modern economy that we hardly think of the central role it plays in our global society. To illustrate the importance and progress of transportation, while a few hundred years ago it took man two days to travel 55 miles, now a car can travel the same distance in only an hour. This improvement in travel speed has economic payback, but also societal benefits.

The construction of transportation infrastructure can be traced as far back as 4000 BC with the discovery of stone-paved streets in the city of Ur in the Middle East, and the corduroy roads found in Glastonbury, England. It was, however, the ability of the Roman Empire to build straight and strong paved roads throughout Europe and North Africa in support of its military crusades that really progressed transportation infrastructure. In more recent times, roads and highways have benefited from the development of tar macadam (the precursor to highway asphalt), which has lead to the construction of the myriad of highways and road systems that are now globally observed.

Initially, the gains from road development were only reaped by the military, but it was not long before benefits from the progress in transportation infrastructure were felt in other walks of life. Transportation infrastructure such as roads, railways, and seaports have facilitated both *agglomeration* (the tendency for a region to have an absolute dominance in an area of economic activity), and *specialization* (a relative concept concerned with the tendency for a region when compared to other regions to produce more of one commodity relative to other commodities). Specialization and

EXHIBIT 2.1   Nations with largest infrastructure stock

	Land area sq km	Population	Population density Pop/sq km	GDP/ capita USD PPP	Urban pop %	Urban pop	Ave urban pop per sq mile	Infra-structure stock (USD trn)	Infra stock/ land sq km USD	Infra stock/ head of pop USD	Infra stock in PPP (US = 100) USD PPP bn
Brazil	8,456,510	198,739,269	24	10,100	86%	170,915,771	16,200	0.6	71	3.0	2.8
China	9,326,410	1,338,612,968	144	6,000	43%	575,603,576	19,800	1.6	172	1.2	12.5
France	640,053	64,057,792	100	32,700	77%	49,324,500	5,900	0.8	1,250	12.5	1.1
Germany	357,021	82,329,758	231	34,800	74%	60,924,021	5,900	0.9	2,521	10.9	1.2
Italy	301,230	58,126,212	193	31,000	68%	39,525,824	5,900	0.6	1,992	10.3	0.9
Japan	377,835	127,078,679	336	34,200	66%	83,871,928	10,400	3.3	8,734	26.0	4.5
Russia	17,075,200	140,041,247	8	15,800	73%	102,230,110	11,900	0.6	35	4.3	1.8
United Kingdom	244,820	61,113,205	250	36,600	90%	55,001,885	10,200	0.6	2,451	9.8	0.8
United States	9,826,630	307,212,123	31	47,000	82%	251,913,941	2,300	4.7	478	15.3	4.7
India	3,287,590	1,166,079,217	355	2,800	29%	338,162,973	38,400		0	0.0	0.0
WORLD					53.8%	2,913,000,000					

Source: RREEF Research & David Kerr, 2008.

agglomeration then enable firms, industries, regions, and even nations to take advantage of first nature advantages and subsequently economies of scale. With the development of comprehensive road systems for instance, sectors such as agriculture were then able to expand their markets beyond that of local subsistence and create a surplus business. Road networks allowed products to be distributed quickly, efficiently, and at a cheaper cost due to smaller transportation costs and smaller production costs. The same benefits have occurred for regions that specialize in a number of other sectors such as manufacturing and service industries.

In facilitating agglomeration and specialization, transportation development has also arguably assisted technological innovations through the act of knowledge spillovers. Economists Marshall (1890), Arrow (1962), and Romer (1986) predicted that knowledge spillovers occur predominantly between firms in a specific industry and that geographically concentrated industries will assist these spillovers and thus stimulate growth. This prediction asserts that knowledge is transferred more effectively between firms within an industry through spying, imitation, lack of property rights, and inter-firm movement; thus ideas are quickly disseminated among neighboring firms. It is regarded that neighboring firms can learn from each other much better than geographically isolated firms. For example, Silicon Valley is comprised of an agglomeration of microchip manufacturers. As a consequence of gossip, products being reverse engineered and employees moving between firms there is a vast spillover of knowledge that results in substantial technological innovations.

Total renewable water resources cu km	Elec product bn kWh	Oil Prod bbl/day	Nat gas prod cu m	Airports paved #	Pipelines km	Railways km	Roadways km	Waterways km	Ports/ terminals #
8,233	437	2,277,000	9,800,000,000	734	19,289	29,295	1,751,868	50,000	7
2,829	3,256	3,725,000	69,270,000,000	413	58,082	75,438	1,930,544	110,000	8
189	570	71,400	953,000,000	295	22,804	29,370	951,500	8,501	9
188	595	148,100	17,960,000,000	331	31,586	48,215	644,480	7,467	8
175	292	166,600	9,706,000,000	101	18,785	19,460	487,700	2,400	8
430	1,195	132,400	3,729,000,000	144	4,082	23,474	1,196,999	1,770	10
4,498	1,016	9,980,000	654,000,000,000	596	246,982	87,157	933,000	102,000	8
161	371	1,690,000	72,300,000,000	312	12,759	16,567	398,366	3,200	10
3,069	4,167	8,457,000	545,900,000,000	5,146	793,285	226,612	6,465,799	41,009	10
1,908	665	880,500	31,700,000,000	251	22,773	63,221	3,316,452	14,500	9

This chapter analyzes the different transportation infrastructure systems in place throughout the globe. It begins with an overview of the current stock of infrastructure projects and infrastructure financing mechanisms in different nations. From this data, we can determine a few conclusions regarding infrastructure spending as a function of population density. The chapter then transitions to an examination of different public private partnership solutions employed in the various transportation infrastructure subsectors, and finishes with a summary of each subsector.

CURRENT STOCK OF INFRASTRUCTURE

A study by Deutsche Bank's alternatives fund manager RREEF calculated a global infrastructure stock of around $20 to $22 trillion (see Exhibit 2.1).

While these broad-based estimates provide a general overview of the market, they fail to address the following issues:

1. How should the cost of infrastructure be accounted for, including the cost of replacing existing assets or the cost of new installation? Nations that installed infrastructure early, such as the United Kingdom, have had the advantage of using that infrastructure for a longer period of time, as opposed to other nations listed in the table. The cost of rebuilding such infrastructure in densely populated countries would be higher than accounted for in this analysis.

2. What is the cost/benefit of the infrastructure investment? Potentially, a lower level of investment may be used more productively and a higher level of investment may be less productive (and considered overinvestment, such as in Japan). *Gold plating* infrastructure, or the obverse of not building long-term infrastructure, is difficult to measure in such a study.
3. What is the correlation between the density of population and level of investment in infrastructure projects? Higher density populations suggest the need for higher cost infrastructure solutions (i.e., more tunneling work needed in urban areas, retrofitting required, and work around existing traffic).

What we do know is that the present global population of around 6.3 billion people is projected to rise to 9.1 billion by 2050. On the face value of this data, one can project a need for around $10 trillion in new infrastructure over the next 40 years (on a per head basis). This does not include the necessary investment to replace, upgrade, and maintain the existing $20 trillion stock. We will assess government ability to pay for such investment in a future chapter.

INFRASTRUCTURE FINANCING MECHANISMS IN DIFFERENT NATIONS

Japan has by far the greatest cost of infrastructure per head of population ($25,990). This may be related to the high cost of land, resulting in the need for higher cost construction solutions (due to population density). The more typical range of infrastructure per head of population for a developed countries stock of infrastructure would be between $10,000 and $15,000. This covers the United States and the larger western European countries.

When looking at other statistics on the same measure of infrastructure stock by country (see Exhibit 2.1), some other trends also appear. Looking at infrastructure by area of the country measured, one can see that Japan has by far the largest stock/sq km, followed by the United Kingdom and Germany. This may support the argument that infrastructure in densely populated countries is more expensive to construct and maintain.

Infrastructure stock by head of population indicates that Japan is again out in front, but this time followed by the United States. Russia performs relatively poorly under both measures.

Thirdly, on the basis of purchasing power parity, utilizing GDP data, China has in relative terms by far the largest stock of infrastructure (almost three times the stock of Japan or the United States). If this measurement is valid, it would suggest that the lower cost of constructing infrastructure in China would allow them around 11 times the nominal product. This would seem to exaggerate the effect of a lower cost base, as many inputs (power turbines, for example) are not 1/12th the cost of the equivalent in the West.

It is difficult to determine what the "right" level of infrastructure stock is for a country. The right level is presumably the most cost-effective infrastructure that gives the optimum level of return, both financial and socially. Results are also affected by population density, with presumably larger countries and widespread populations needing a larger infrastructure capital stock. However, general conclusions that can be reached are that Japan has a relatively high stock of infrastructure, considering its lower economic growth rate at present. China has a reasonable level of infrastructure, but requires more, particularly because of its high rate of economic growth.

PUBLIC-PRIVATE PARTNERSHIP SOLUTIONS

Public-private partnerships (PPPs) have a number of potential solutions and methods of cooperation between the public sector and the private sector. Listed in Exhibit 2.2 are some of the different structures.

PPP structures share risk between the public authority and the private company, with typically the private sector being held to quality of service criteria and fulfilling a price objective (either highest price paid or lowest cost of service to the public).

The use of private sector capital in financing infrastructure has been common practice for many years. The electricity utilities in the United States, the water and wastewater companies in France, and privately owned ports are just a few examples of privately financed infrastructure that have been in existence for more than 100 years. Transportation is perhaps the most difficult sector to draw solely private capital without subsidy of government involvement. Transportation is an essential part of a widely functioning economy, and society has become used to funding transportation links not necessarily through direct payment for use, but through a widely drawn taxation system, which is then channeled by government toward projects identified by the administration or other societal bodies. This has led to a bias toward new construction projects over maintenance projects, due to the political benefits of construction employment and clear political benefits in exhibiting the new assets brought about by the investment. Over time, the maintenance backlog of infrastructure stock has tended to outpace the

EXHIBIT 2.2 Different Structures for Public-Private Partnerships

Form of Privatization	Duration (years)	Financial transactions within the contract	Criteria for awarding the contract	Scope of regulation
Service contract	<5 years	Fixed service fee	Technical prequalification; lowest fee	Quality of service and maintenance
Management contract	<10	Private operator receives a service fee	Technical prequalification; lowest service fee	Quality of service and maintenance
Lease contract	6–10	Operator pays rental fee	Technical prequalification; highest rental	Quality of service and maintenance and tariffs
Concession	15–50	Operator retains all of the tariff revenue stream	Technical prequalification; management expertise	Quality of service and maintenance and tariffs
Build-Own-Transfer/ Build-Transfer-Operate	20–40	Operator receives the revenue stream	Technical prequalification; lowest service fee	Quality of service and maintenance
Build-Own-Operate	Life of assets	Operator receives the revenue stream	Quality of projects; lowest service fee	Quality of service and maintenance
Private sale	25–99	Private operator purchases the state assets	Technical prequalification; lowest service fee or highest upfront price	Quality of service and maintenance and tariffs
Flotation	Indefinite	Public purchases shares of the floated utility	n/a	Quality of service and maintenance and tariffs

publicly available funding for its execution. Some basic examples of maintenance backlog in the United States include:

- 3.9 million miles of roads and highways
- 5,400 public airports
- 3,600 water port terminals
- 200,000 miles of freight and passenger railroad track

The rest of the chapter proceeds to break down the state of fundraising and project development for each of the different subsectors within transportation. The key findings for each are summarized here:

- **Highways and bridges.** Funding is being squeezed on both state and federal levels as both maintenance and replacement costs rise.
- **Automotive.** Miles traveled have increased 95 percent since 1980, but road capacity has risen only 4 percent. Increasing congestion and increasing commute and transit times (damaging aggregate productivity).
- **Aviation.** Approximately 60 percent of global air traffic passes through U.S. airspace on a daily basis, utilizing the same traffic management (ATM) system that dates back to the 1950s.
- **Rail.** A significant share of the nation's freight is carried by rail—a system in need of modernization and better integration with the nation's ports, highways, and trucks.

The estimated capital requirement for the period from 2005 to 2025 is $286 billion. Over and above the capital requirement for infrastructure, as of 2009, state budget gaps for 2010 to 2011 alone are cumulatively $452 billion according to the Center on Budget and Policy Priorities. This growth in maintenance backlog and decreasing ability to fund the necessary work can be replicated in most countries around the world.

Highways and Bridges

Toll roads and bridges have been in existence for centuries. Currently, the United States, France, Spain, and Italy operate the most extensive networks of toll roads. Mexico, Chile, and many other countries (especially in Europe) have direct pay toll systems, while still others have a vignette system. Austria and Switzerland are examples of countries who use a vignette, where the right to use the highway is purchased and displayed through a windshield sticker. The initiation of these structures has offered multiple benefits to society. The U.S. Federal Highway Administration calculated that there have been three principal areas of national benefit to the development of the highway network:

1. **Industry cost savings.** Estimated industrial cost savings at 18 cents per year for each dollar invested in the roads system, calculated over the 1950–1989 period.
2. **Productivity growth.** In the period 1980–1989, highway capital investments are estimated to have contributed 7 percent to 8 percent to annual productivity growth.
3. **Social return.** The net social rate of return for the highways system was estimated to be 16 percent per annum.

How these benefits are calculated is unclear, however they should be taken at face value as an attempt to capture the social benefits that accrue through increased ease of transporting goods and services through a highway and bridge/tunnel system.

Construction and maintenance costs for the U.S. interstate highways are funded by approximately 70 percent user fees, principally through gasoline taxes. The balance of around 30 percent of funds comes from general fund receipts, bond issues, designated property, and other taxes. The Federal Highway Trust Fund (FHTF) is federally mandated and is used to ensure dependable financing of maintenance of the interstate highway system, principally through gasoline taxes. The Congressional Budget Office estimates that the FHTF will have a balance of roughly $3 billion at the end of 2010— less than 30 days' spending during summer months.

There are many PPP alternatives available (refer back to Exhibit 2.2). The mechanisms for delivery of new roads include full tolling and shadow tolling. The viability of full tolling for a greenfield road is questionable, as the risk is relatively high that usage will not be insufficient. Allowing the private sector to build and toll however has been used successfully, notably in Australia. Usage risk is generally beyond the control of the private sector to mitigate or accurately measure. Shadow tolling regimes allow the private sector to take the cost of delivery risk as well as a limited amount of usage risk. The public benefit that accrues from the construction of new roads may make the public sector willing to take this risk, as other long-term benefits may accrue from the provision of a new road. Shadow tolls are calibrated such that the government will have a scheduled payment rate for each vehicle that uses the road. The first vehicle will entail a relatively high payment, such that a very conservative traffic projection will ensure coverage of operating costs along with the debt raised to build the road. Payments above this level will become less per unit, such that the equity returns will be limited to a predefined level; therefore, equity will take a limited downside on usage (as opposed to taking the full risk of usage in a full toll road). Shadow tolling has been used in Poland, Austria, and the United Kingdom as a mechanism to allow government to continue to control whether road usage is tolled, and at what level that toll may be. The right to toll and adjust charges for road usage is a public policy issue, and, importantly to the private sector participant, will affect usage patterns (the higher the charge the less likely a road is to be used). See Case Study 1, A1 Motorway, Gdansk—Torun, Poland, at the end of this chapter.

Existing roads have from time-to-time been sold by the public sector owner through a concession or long-term lease to the private sector. For the most part, this practice has been limited to within the United States, with prominent examples being the Indiana Toll Road and Chicago Skyway. In these instances, the private sector paid an upfront amount to the public sector for the use of the assets. The private sector then took the risk that the predefined toll schedule and their expectations of future traffic growth would be sufficient to pay operating costs as well as pay back the debt financing they raised, plus pay their equity investors back and provide a return on the investment.

Railways

Rail systems play a dual role of moving passengers and freight around, achieving both these objectives in a fairly energy efficient way. Due to the fixed capital stock, they are capital intensive and relatively inflexible modes of transport relative to the road network. Due to their capacity to move large amounts of freight over long distances in a timely and cost effective way, railways are an integral part of the logistics chain in moving goods from one market to another.

Passenger rail is presently very difficult, if not impossible, to run without a public subsidy. Most passenger rail systems struggle to cover operating costs through the ticket price, which leaves the repayment of construction and maintenance of the system to be paid by others (typically government). Freight rail can be economically viable in its own right, depending on the system, how it is integrated and obligated to passenger rail, and demand by freight shippers. The integration of passenger rail with freight rail in Europe has made it difficult for the private sector to play a meaningful role in operations. The United Kingdom has franchised out passenger rail operations, with performance standards being designated for all bidders and a substantial subsidy ultimately being paid for the operation of the franchise. Operations tend to be undertaken by the private sector, most of whom are listed companies.

The United States and Canada have substantial privately owned rail networks. The key difference with Europe is that the infrastructure is owned by the rail operators, who can determine priority rights to the track between freight and passenger demands. In Europe, passenger rail has priority, but in North America, where freight traffic is substantial and profitable, freight can have priority. This priority is attractive to freight customers, as time-to-market is important in their business. Therefore, the share of freight carried by rail in North America is markedly greater than that in Europe, and the economic viability to North American freight rail is stronger than that of its European counterparts.

The principal source of revenue for railways is through cargo shipment fees and passenger ticket fares. For most, if not all, passenger railways, a public subsidy is required. As indicated here, the infrastructure may be owned by the state, which can also provide the rail service, or outsource its provision to the private sector. In North America, access to track can be charged, with the private sector owner charging other operators to access its rail.

Seaports

Seaports are another key node in the shipment of goods from one market to another. Seaports require specialized equipment for loading and unloading, which depends on the mode of transportation employed by the sea carrier and rail carrier. Break-bulk mode tends to be used for loose commodities, such as coal. Liquids, such as oil or liquefied natural gas, require specialized handling equipment and vessels. Many goods are transported today in containers, modularizing transportation by standardizing and thus simplifying the loading, unloading and transportation process for both the shipping and rail industries.

Revenues at seaports tend to come from handling charges billed to the steamship company. Operational efficiency and consequent cost effectiveness are critical to the economic viability of a cargo port; by minimizing yard handling or providing more attractive operating features, an operator can reduce costs. Cost reduction, in turn, either increases profitability or helps to reduce charges to customers.

Cargo port terminals are privately owned and/or operated in many locations. Large operators, such as Port of Singapore Authority International, Dubai Ports World, and Hutchison Port Holdings are international independent port operators, with numerous operating locations around the world. Some terminals are operated by divisions of large steamship lines, such as AP Moller Container Terminals and COSCO Terminals. Traditionally, these steamship line operators may not have been focused on maximizing container terminal profits in their own right, instead of acting as a cost center for the steamship lines operations. However, there is some evidence that this approach may now be changing in favor of being a stand-alone profit center, as the independent operators manage their business as profit centers.

The steady increase in global trade since the 1970s saw the value of cargo ports increase markedly in recent years. The sharp global contraction since late 2007 has however seen global trade sink sharply. This reduction in trade volumes has had a consequent impact on the value of cargo ports.

Airports

Airports are a principal entry and exit point for passenger and cargo traffic that are transported by commercial aircraft. Almost all airports have historically been developed by the public sector, although some have now been leased out or sold to the private sector, which is then responsible for operations, maintenance, and development of the assets. For example, the British Airports Authority is owned by a private sector consortium, Auckland Airport is publicly listed, and Frankfurt Airport is a past publicly listed firm. Europe and Australia have a number of privately owned and/or operated airports, including Copenhagen, Brussels, and all the major airports in Australia. The United States' and Canada's commercial airports are generally operated by the public sector.

An airport's revenue streams come from both regulated and nonregulated activities. Regulated activities will tend to have a minimum service requirement and an absolute safety requirement relative to their provision. Regulated activities cover services to airlines, and may include:

- Passenger facility charges, which are added directly to the passenger's ticket price.
- Aircraft parking charges, for aircraft waiting time on the airport apronway (which is akin to an aircraft parking space).
- Take-off and landing charges, for runway use.
- Aerobridge charges, for the time spent using passenger loading bridges.
- Support services, including fueling, ground handling and such like.
- Cargo and freight charges for the loading, unloading, and handling of air cargo.

Nonregulated revenues cover activities not essential to commercial airport and airline safety. Nonregulated revenues may include:

- Retail, from duty-free shopping and other commercial retail outlets.
- Food and beverage, from rental and revenue sharing agreements with food and beverage outlets.
- Real estate, from rental and sales of real estate around or within the boundaries of the airport.

The marked increase in passenger traffic since the 1970s has made airports an attractive investment opportunity, with prices increasing sharply over the period up to 2007. The 2007 financial markets crisis followed by the global contraction has caused a reduction in passenger numbers at some airports. It is possible that pricing will be affected by this passenger reduction, dampening investment prospects. See Case Study 2, London Luton Airport, at the end of this chapter.

CASE STUDIES

Case Study 1: A1 Motorway, Gdansk—Torun, Poland

The A1 Motorway in Poland runs 560 km from Gdansk on the northern Baltic coast of Poland to Cieszyn in the southern Polish border. Poland had not developed a significant motorway system up through the 1990s. Due to severe budget constraints, the Polish Government bid out much of the financing, construction, and operation of the motorway system in 1997.

However, the bids were solicited as Build-Operate-Transfer (BOT) projects, with the private sector required to take motorway traffic risk—their only source of revenue would be tolls from the vehicles that used the motorway.

At that time, tolling risk proved to be unfinanceable. Poland did not have a history of how drivers would react to having to pay tolls to use a new road, and financiers were concerned that usage would be too low to support the initial repayment of costs for the project. Recent history at that time showed this to be a reasonable assessment in former Communist countries in Eastern Europe. For instance Hungary had also undertaken rapid development of transportation infrastructure to boost its economy. The Hungarian M1/M15 toll motorway was the first to be implemented in Central and Eastern Europe. Although the project was completed on schedule and on budget in 1995, initial traffic volumes were reportedly around 40 percent lower than anticipated. Higher tolls did not compensate for the lower volume, and instead led to greater public dissatisfaction. The project for the PPP ultimately had to be taken over by the government, with the cost to the public purse defeating the initial rationale.

Financiers for the A1 Motorway required that the government take some of the key risks related to traffic volume. The private sector could then be given a more limited downside, which particularly favored the lenders who provided lower cost funding, while equity investors returns were capped on the upside. The financing of Phase 1 of the A1 Motorway, from Gdansk to

Nowe Marzy, was completed in 2005, and construction of the remainder was completed by end 2008. With approximately one-fifth of the 568 km motorway completed at the beginning of 2009, a contract was signed for the construction of a 180 km stretch from Strykow to Pyrzowice. This section of the highway will be built within a PPP framework by Autostrada Poludnie with construction work beginning in 2009.

The A1 Motorway process provided several key takeaways, which include:

- **Timely Legislation.** It is surprising how many PPP processes start without adequate legislation in place. The attitude seems to be that the public sector will fill in the gaps later if the private sector shows it really needs something. However, time is money and filling in the gaps can take time. Key PPP legislation relating to the A1 Motorway was missing in 1997 and had to be enacted after the bids were received. The processing of this legislation was time consuming and, ultimately, the Concession Agreement was initialed in 2002 and signed in 2004. It took seven years to finalize documentation from when negotiations began.
- **Affordability.** The initially proposed scope for the project had a project cost of over $1.2 billion. This came to almost 1 percent of the national GDP in the mid 1990s. As a consequence, and after protracted negotiations, construction of the motorway was split into two sections. This action phased the funding of the project and made the project more affordable. The phasing of the project also allowed traffic usage of the first phase to be assessed prior to making the commitment to fund the second section of the motorway.
- **Patient Partnering.** Development of infrastructure is a costly and time-consuming business. The seven-year period to arrive at a signed concession agreement cost the private sector participants many millions of dollars, which would be paid back only if the project was successful. It also ensured that the private sector partners tied up important resources to work on trying to resolve key hurdles to the projects implementation, including legislative issues. At many points in the seven-year period, it looked like the project would be cancelled. As a consequence of the extended period of time between original award and concession signature, the original equity group changed substantially. Of the original Bechtel, Bank Gospodarki Zywnosciowej, Gdansk Przedsiebiorstwo Robot Drogowych and Intertoll group, only Intertoll remained after seven years at financial close (when money was available for construction to begin). In the instance of the A1 Motorway, the delays to project implementation were ultimately not fatal to the project itself. However, there was

the risk that delays would cause the partnership element of the PPP to
break down.

■ **Low Cost of Funding.** PPPs tend to be benchmarked for value using a
public sector comparator (PSC). The PSC measures whether a private
sector proposal offers value for money when compared with the most
efficient form of public sector procurement. Therefore, the ability to
raise low-cost debt funding is critical to project viability. For lenders
to take project-specific risk in a low-cost way (rather than lend against
a broad government tax base), some of the key project risks need to
be appropriately allocated to those best positioned to manage them.
To this end, the need for the government to mitigate traffic risk was
critical for the participation of international lenders. Ultimately, the
Polish Government agreed to establish a shadow toll regime for the
motorway, where tolls would not be directly charged by the private
sector. A shadow toll is paid by the government to the A1 concessionaire,
which allows security of payment to lenders and maintains future tolling
of motorways in Poland under the aegis of the government, who can
decide on its potential implementation as a matter of coordinated public
policy.

Case Study 2: London Luton Airport

London Luton Airport is located 30 miles north of London and is one
of five airports that principally serve the metropolitan London area, the
others being Heathrow, Gatwick, Stansted, and London City. Heathrow,
Gatwick, and Stansted have been owned by British Airports Authority
(BAA), although Gatwick has been sold to a third party in 2009. In
2006, the five London airports served around 135 million passengers,
with BAA having the dominant position of serving around 92 percent of
those passengers. The position of London Luton in 1997, when it was bid
under a concession agreement, was even weaker. London Luton carried
around 2.6 million passengers, mostly package holiday passengers and
was not able to build a strong momentum in the London area travel
market. Package holiday passengers don't travel on schedule air services,
but on flights for their specific vacation that tend to be organized by tour
operators.

Luton Borough Council held a competition to determine the private
sector partner to further develop the airport over the proceeding 30 years
and potentially longer. The private sector would guarantee the construction
of a new terminal building, improve airport infrastructure, develop airline
traffic, expand upon the commercial capabilities at the airport, and further
develop the airport as an economic hub for the Luton area.

The status of the airport prior to the PPP:

- The airport was wholly owned by Luton Borough Council and managed by the public sector.
- The airport was marginally profitable, and made little return back to its owner.
- The asset base comprised outdated infrastructure, with aged buildings, terminal, and airport apronways.
- Operating over capacity limits with an aging terminal designed for under 3 million passengers, leading to customer dissatisfaction and inability to grow.

This led to a need for capital investment. However, government-imposed restrictions on local council borrowing ensured the needed capital investment wasn't possible.

After PPP:

- There was a 30-year concession with private sector partners, who changed the management of the airport and its objectives.
- A new terminal building was constructed, with a capacity up to 10 million passengers, allowing business expansion and improving the customer experience.
- The airport's customer base was diversified, with the introduction of new airlines, improving business performance.
- GBP 110 million in capital investment was undertaken over five years.
- The expansion was financed with no recourse to the council, therefore their financial liability was mitigated.
- Council revenues from the airport greatly enhanced, with percentage of revenues paid to them. Consequently, the council essentially received a new source of revenue.

Strategy

Capital improvements increased the attractiveness of the airport. A new terminal was constructed, existing terminal improved and refurbished, taxiways were extended and widened, the number of runway exits increased, aircraft stands were constructed, new car parks were built, and airport access roads reconstructed. These improvements improved the customer experience at the airport.

Strategically positioned the airport. London Luton Airport needed to establish a sustainable position for itself where the very large airports in its market would be less able to use their dominant position to erode its market share. London Luton Airport attracted new customers to the airport. This greatly improved passenger growth numbers, enhancing profitability.

Maximize the use of the limited Luton Airport site. The airport has a relatively small footprint, which required that maximum utilization of the asset was essential to make best use of the commercial opportunities that come from airport operations. Through smart capital spending, phased appropriately to demand requirements, the airport was able to achieve this.

London Luton has thrived under the PPP, growing from 2.6 million passengers in 1997 to 10.2 million in 2008.

CHAPTER 3

Energy Infrastructure and the Industrialization of Emerging Markets

Framework for Private Sector Investment

Wilbur L. Ross
CEO, WL Ross & Co.

Zhongmin Shen
Head of Private Equity—China, Invesco

Brian Foerster
Capital Markets Analyst, Invesco

E nergy infrastructure plays a dynamic role in the economies of emerging market countries. By virtue of their "emerging" status, growing from a closed or impoverished state toward a developed market, these countries are at an in-between maturing stage. To become a developed nation, energy and transportation are essential to the goals of industrialization and sustainable economic growth. Today's emerging market countries will either evolve into fully developed markets or continue to face headwinds due to the numerous challenges and risks they face. To ascertain the most attractive infrastructure investment opportunities and risks inherent in emerging market countries, we need first to understand what characterizes such a country:

- High and/or accelerating economic growth
- Improving political and social conditions

- Increasing privatization and economic liberalization
- Growing trade and demand for goods
- Maturing legal and regulatory systems

Governments have long been the sole or dominant provider of financing for infrastructure investment and development, to varying degrees of success. Today, as governments find themselves increasingly constrained in their spending, either due to macroeconomic turmoil or political pressures, the private sector has become a significantly larger participant in the financing and execution of infrastructure projects. And more specifically, demand among investors has shifted from developed markets to emerging and maturing ones, where potential long-term returns are more attractive.

One of the most significant risks for infrastructure investors in emerging markets is the political complexity of the projects unique to each country. In China, for example, state-owned enterprises (SOEs)—businesses and manufacturers subsidized by the government—have highly favorable access to state financing for projects. By contrast, non-SOEs are virtually unable to participate in the financing or approval for new projects. This business environment makes investment in infrastructure projects highly dependent on having established partnerships with SOEs and a positive relationship with regulatory entities. This example of a formerly closed society in China taking incremental steps toward free market capitalism, preserving some state control of economic activity while liberalizing other facets, is common in the investment profile of emerging market economies. For external investors, therefore, success in this environment is closely correlated with access to capital, access to government regulators and key business participants, and a local expertise in the country and region to manage risk and identify growth opportunities.

We will look briefly at the history of infrastructure in emerging markets, and then focus on the current boom in spending on energy infrastructure expansion. Looking specifically at India (early), China (maturing), and South Korea (developed), we will examine three distinct stages of an infrastructure expansion. Lastly, we will estimate what the future of infrastructure in emerging markets will look like, particularly from the private sector perspective, and where the opportunities and risks are for investors.

HISTORICAL PERSPECTIVE OF ENERGY INFRASTRUCTURE IN EMERGING MARKETS

When the United States was an emerging market country, coal power, steam power, and the build-out of a national electrical grid accompanied the construction of interstate railroads in our industrial revolution. The pay-off to investing in these structures came in a number of ways: social (the improvement of people's standard of living, comfort, and livelihoods); economic (facilitating commerce and growth of the capital base); and political (liberalizing markets increases trade, facilitates inclusion in the global community, and can open previously closed societies).

The United States expanded its infrastructure both during boom economic times (post-reconstruction) and during its worst economic environment (New Deal investments during the Depression). Similarly today, in large part due to the economic downturn and some highly publicized structural failures, the United States is increasing its infrastructure investment again, but today as the world's largest economy. Investments such as these in a highly developed country are typically low-medium return opportunities, focused on replenishing aged assets rather than focusing the bulk of development on new technologies that meet new demand.

Following the fall of the Soviet Union, the success of Japan's booming capitalist economy in the 1980s, and the concurrent democratization of many large Latin American and Asian countries, economic growth flourished during the 1990s in many countries that had previously been under state-controlled rule. There was a wide range of sustainability and economic stability in these newly liberalized markets. Countries such as South Korea flourished due to a well-organized regulatory environment and a well-established capitalist regime. Russia, by contrast, saw enormous growth rates due to pent-up demand and newfound economic opportunity offset by a lack of government transparency, widespread business corruption, and a lack of infrastructure beyond its major cities.

By the end of the 1990s and into the new century, emerging markets best positioned for growth in infrastructure were primarily in Asia. Political and economic liberalizations combined with a demographic shift from agrarian-based economies to industrial-based ones created a favorable environment for investment in new technologies that improve the aggregate standard of living. Energy, power, and transportation are the primary components of these efforts, which include:

- Expanding the power grid to large segments of these countries that were previously without power
- Developing rapid transit and greater access to urban and commerce centers
- Building more efficient, less expensive, and more environmentally sound sources of mass-produced power

ENERGY INFRASTRUCTURE—ASIA'S GROWTH ENGINE AT THREE STAGES

In North America, Western Europe, Japan, and Australia, demand has risen significantly in recent years for the replenishment on aging assets. While this demand necessitates investment to sustain the efficacy of these economies and the wealth creation and standard of living for the populations of these countries, these are very mature economies, which have strong internal competition for infrastructure projects, driving down investment margins. In addition, the late-stage nature of the projects themselves, primarily the renewal of old assets with higher cost new assets, offers less attractive opportunities for return on private investment.

Consequently, the focus of many investors pursuing infrastructure opportunities has been on emerging market countries. In particular, this focus has turned largely to countries in Asia, where accelerated economic growth has driven demographic shifts from agrarian professions to higher wage and higher margin professions in industry and services. Much of this attention has focused in particular on the dramatic urbanization and industrialization of India, China, and South Korea. These three countries can also provide an example of early-, mid-, and late-stage characteristics of emerging market infrastructure development. South Korea is a prime example of a country that has successfully utilized government and private sector investment to expand its industrial infrastructure to meet urbanization and demographic changes. Primarily due to its long-standing democracy, well-established legal and regulatory regime, and relatively mature capital markets, its infrastructure expansion was largely successful from an operational standpoint and for investors. China's economic emergence remains at an earlier stage, though high growth rates and urbanization trends over the past decade have accelerated their ability to attract investment and fund a large-scale transformation of its energy and transportation infrastructure. India, by comparison, is at a more nascent stage as an emerging market opportunity for investment, as it is faced with the challenges of a cumbersome regulatory and legal environment for business, as well as substantial funding needs to meet its wide-ranging infrastructure needs. (See Exhibit 3.1.)

INFRASTRUCTURE CHARACTERISTICS

Early stage investment opportunities include "Greenfield" projects such as new road, bridge, and tunnel developments, or assets in higher risk locations or where there are no established demand patterns that can be relied on. There will be little or no income from the asset for some significant period of time.

Growth stage investments include expansion projects and new privatizations of existing operating assets. With these assets, there are established operating results that can be analyzed and reliable forecasts that can allow for some view of potential operating growth. In this stage of development, the asset should deliver a reasonably consistent yield with attractive growth underpinning future results.

Late stage infrastructure assets are considered mature, proven assets. Here, usage of the road, airport, utility, or other facility will be well-established and income will be the predominant component of the investment return. In many cases, particularly in the utilities field, infrastructure businesses are regulated, with price increases on their product limited to periodic government review. Asset maturity typically occurs when monopoly-like conditions exist, providing for predictable income streams for investors.

THE INVESTMENT OPPORTUNITY: EMERGING MARKET INFRASTRUCTURE SUPPLY SHORTAGE

In each of these countries, pressure on government budgets has made private investment a necessity to fulfill the demand and aspirations for infrastructure development, though for different reasons. In South Korea, which is further along than China or India in its growth phase, enormous investment over the past two decades in infrastructure has recently been reduced sharply as greater emphasis on social welfare and health care has taken precedence over further government expenditure on new assets. This evolution has subsequently prompted the Korean government to actively seek out private investors for ongoing projects. In India and China, the enormous budget deficits incurred by both governments, despite their rapid growth, has forced both to create substantial provisions for outside private investment.[1]

Shortage of financing for infrastructure projects, thus, provides one of the primary impetuses—and opportunities—for investment in this region. Moreover, a private investor with an expertise in a specific type of infrastructure project such as building airports, possessing the knowledge and ability to manage the regulatory aspects, costs, and profitable execution of a project would be able to generate potentially outsized returns in an emerging market country in dire need of an airport to service its surging need for air travel.

EXHIBIT 3.1 Sample Characteristics of Infrastructure Assets, Emerging and Developed Markets

	India	China	Developed World
Stage of development	Early-mid	Mid	Late
Investability	Mid	Low	High
Where are the funds being raised	Unlisted, targeted funds Development organizations Governments	Local firms Chinese listed entities • National/provincial/ private partnership arrangements	Listed infrastructure funds Listed generalist funds Unlisted funds Listed, international firms Pension funds Governments
Ownership and regulations	Full ownership available, but confusing regulatory overlap causes uncertainty	Ownership is largely restricted, with an authoritative regulatory environment. The government is heavy-handed with land acquisition	Full ownership available, with any restrictions made clear
How safe is your investment?	Significant court delays, democratic bureaucracy and restrictive labor laws mean unpredictable outcomes	Threats of sector nationalism are low, and protection of assets held jointly with government is high	Well-developed legal frameworks, open financial systems, and political stability provide a high degree of certainty

Source: Macquarie Research, Invesco Private Capital, "The Opportunity in Global Infrastructure Investment," July 2008.

There are common areas of infrastructure investment in Korea, India, and China that will require billions of dollars in both Greenfield and middle-stage projects. Transportation, power, and energy comprise the most important aspects of an emerging market's growing infrastructure demand. Unlike most developed countries, where roads, rails, airports, seaports, utilities, power companies, and coal/oil production are embedded and wired into people's daily lives, these infrastructure assets are often sparsely centered in countries that have only a handful of urban centers and a dominant agrarian population. As countries such as India and China in recent years commit to a rapid expansion of their economy, implementing infrastructure essentials of developed nations fosters its own embedded growth engine, and thus provides an attractive opportunity to private investors.

Looking at India and China, the two largest emerging market economies and populations, there are enormous market-driven needs for infrastructure investment and government commitments that will require billions of dollars per project of private investment.

India

India's investment in its infrastructure has expanded in recent years, but has failed to keep pace with the strong economic growth over the past decade. The World Bank forecasts that India's infrastructure investment will require $425 billion within the next 5 to 10 years to address both the population growth in the country and the growth of industry. Top among priorities is the need for electricity countrywide, followed by roads, telecommunications, and railway.[2]

India's government (The GoI) is well aware of the need for infrastructure investment from the private sector and has actively encouraged private equity investors to take part in many projects. Of top concern is the lagging power supply to the Indian people. While electricity consumption over the past decade has risen 9 percent to 10 percent, capacity has risen only 7 percent per annum. With India expecting energy needs to double by 2020, The GoI is committed to public-private partnerships (PPP) to meet the transmission and distribution goals established in the Electricity Act of 2003.[3] While private investment has risen in these power projects, supply shortages persist due to insufficient infrastructure assets.

Meanwhile, transportation infrastructure that supports globalization in India (airports and seaports) has grown more in line with the country's increasing openness to globalization and trade. The Airports Authority of India Amendment Bill of 2003 paved the way for private investment in the country's airport industry. The country now has over 450 airports managed by various public and private entities, while many of India's airports are also being renovated and upgraded to meet the increasing travel and commercial needs of its population. In addition to high profile renovations of the Delhi and Mumbai airports, whose management was recently shifted from the government to the private sector, India's government has also initiated airport development projects over the past three years to support an additional 37 nonmetro and Greenfield airports, to be developed and managed by private entities. This expansion of airport infrastructure and increased privatization of the industry has of course been driven largely by the rapid emergence of India's airline industry, including the launch of low-cost carriers in recent years.[4]

EXHIBIT 3.2   Road Development Plan: Vision 2021 of Indian Roads Congress

Scheme	2001–2011		2011–2021	
	Length (km)	Amount (Rs billions)	Length (km)	Amount (Rs billions)
Expressways	3,000	300	7,000	700
National Highways	61,000	1,200	62,000	1,300
State Highways	78,000	750	127,000	1,250
Major district roads	100,000	400	130,000	600
Total	242,000	2,650	326,000	3,850

Source: Indian Roads Congress, "Sustainable Transport Development—A Vision," 2001.

India's internal transportation infrastructure is in worse shape, however, with a dire shortage of roads and an enormous ageing rail system in need of significant renewal. With only 55 percent of its roads paved and 1000 km of paved road per million people, India's road infrastructure is one-tenth that of the average for the developed world. To address this problem, the GoI has implemented the National Highway Development Program, which, estimated at $13.2 billion, will require substantial private investment.[5]

Similarly, India's rail system, the second largest in the world at 63,000 km, has received little investment in renewal of assets over the past 50 years. As a result, the Ministry of Railways launched a $3.3 billion program to support and strengthen India's rail system, requiring much of this to be driven by private investment.[6]

China

In China, over 10 million rural citizens have migrated to urban areas each year between 1995–2007,[7] creating massive demand for housing, transportation, communication, education and health care services in cities, which required a huge amount of investment in living facilities and infrastructure. A main contributor to China's strong economic growth—9 percent on average since 1978—has been investment.[8] At an average nominal growth rate of 17 percent per year (prior to the financial market downturn of 2008–2009), investment has on average been contributing 4.0 percentage points to China's GDP growth every year over the past 30 years. After years of rapid growth, investment is now taking the largest share in China's GDP—42 percent in 2007 versus 35 percent for household consumption.

The migration has been accompanied by industrialization, as the migrated labor force—about 70 percent of the migrated population are between the ages of 15 and 64—need to find new jobs in cities. Since each new job requires certain capital expenditure to equip the labor, the industrialization process also requires massive spending on capital equipment and related infrastructure.

With the urbanization ratio expected to rise from 43 percent in 2005 to 47 percent by 2010—as laid out in the People's Republic of China's (PRC's) *Eleventh Five-Year Plan (2006–2010)*—and the total population expected to rise from 1.31 billion to 1.36 billion, about 77 million rural residents are expected to migrate to urban areas during these five years. To accommodate this migrated labor force, the government set a goal of creating 9 million new urban jobs every year between 2005 and 2010. Accomplishing this goal and accommodating the living and space requirements of new urban residents has necessitated massive investment in both infrastructure and capital equipment.

While the PRC's plan requires a vast amount of spending on infrastructure in the next five years, infrastructure investment only accounted for one-third of China's total fixed-asset investment in 2007. Part of the infrastructure investment (such as in highways, railways, airports, and seaports) is done by the private sector (including state-owned and state-controlled enterprises). As a result, the share of the state budget in total fixed-asset investment is very small; it has been less than 5 percent in recent years. In other words, the majority of the investment has been, and will continue to be, done by the private sector. This should create significant business opportunities for private companies in the years to come, not only via direct involvement in investment projects, but also via increased demand for upstream capital goods and raw materials.

In China, the levels of service for many types of infrastructure services are inadequate at interregional, regional, and local rural scales. This is true particularly in the western and central provinces, but also along the coast in low-income regions and in areas that are unprepared for the growing pressures of urbanization. The inadequate levels of service undermine equity and constrain continued economic development.[9]

Despite overcapacity in the manufacturing sectors, China is still facing shortages in many other areas, especially in infrastructure, energy, and natural resources. While China's economic growth benefited hugely from its relatively well-built infrastructure—thanks to massive spending on infrastructure in the past three decades—it is in turn creating even stronger demand for additional infrastructure investments.

Today, shortages are seen in many areas and regions (e.g., in railways, airports, roads and ports; in rural areas and midwestern provinces; and in the services sectors). As a result, infrastructure investments in these areas remain a key focus for the Chinese government, not only today, but also likely over the next decade, as the task to meet the demand will take years to accomplish. Such investments will create massive demand for energy and natural resources in the years to come, adding more pressure to the already tight supply-demand balance in those areas. China's commitment to building this energy and power infrastructure is also focused on cleaner coal and renewable energy to offset both the severe environmental problems in the country and the long-term sustainability of the energy infrastructure. All of these ambitious projects will consequently require enormous private investment, expertise, and innovation.

CHINA'S PUBLIC-PRIVATE OBJECTIVES FOR INVESTING IN RENEWABLE ENERGY

China has become a world leader in wind power turbines and solar panels. The government views these industries as potentially major export businesses in the future. To encourage domestic demand, the power grids are required to accept first all renewable power available to it and to pay a 15 percent premium for it. In addition, the largest power company, Huaneng, is well underway with what is likely the world's most sophisticated combination of coal gasification and carbon sequestration on a commercial scale. Chinese entrepreneurs also are major sellers of carbon credits in the International markets.

These ambitions are due to both practical reasons (lower-cost energy with less dependence on imported resources) and sociopolitical ones (repairing its reputation as a country with dense pollution). In February 2005, the National People's Congress approved the Renewable Energy Law, which first affirmed the strategic policy focus on renewable energy in China. The law not only set development goals for renewable energy, but also stipulated specific measures to reach these goals, such as priority grid access for renewable power developers, feed-in tariffs for renewable electricity, and subsidies for renewable energy.

In order to elaborate further on the direction of renewable energy development and give the market a clearer vision, the National Development and Reform Commission (NDRC) published the Medium and Long-term Development Plan for Renewable Energy in China in August 2007. This plan is the regulation that details the Renewable Energy Law's implementation. It sets renewable energy development goals for 2010 and 2020 at 10 percent and 15 percent of total energy consumption, respectively. The plan also set development goals for key renewable energy sectors and the estimated cost to reach 2020 goals was 2 trillion (RMB Yuan) or $293 billion (USD). Since only a minority portion of the cost will be funded by central and local governments, the plan created an enormous investment opportunity for the private sector.

EXHIBIT 3.3   Government Objectives for Renewable Energy Market Potential

Resources	Objectives by 2010	Objectives by 2020	Market Potential until 2020	Estimated Investment Costs
Hydropower	190GW	300GW	$188 billion	$1,025/kW
Biomass	5.5GW	30GW	27 billion	1,025/kW
Wind	5GW	30GW	29 billion	952/kW
Biogas	40 million household	80 million household	27 billion	439/household
Solar	300MW	1.8GW	19 billion	10,981/kW
Others			3 billion	

Note: Exchange rate: $1(USD) = 6.58RMB.
Source: National Development and Reform Commission.

The study indicated that China has huge untapped potential for wind power. The total technically exploitable wind resources are perhaps as much as 1000GW including 250GW of onshore resources and 750GW of offshore resources.[10] Meanwhile, the total installed wind power generation capacity was 12.21GW in China as the end of 2008. Even though this figure is far ahead of the NDRC's 2010 objective, it is only 1.22 percent of commercial feasible resources, indicating a substantial growth opportunity in the coming future.

In May 2009, the National Energy Administration (NEA), the energy administrative arm of the NDRC, revealed that the development goals for renewable energy will be adjusted shortly. According to the NEA, wind power will be the focus of the renewable energy promotion. The target installed generation capacity for wind power in China by 2020 will be reset to 100GW–150GW, a big boost from the original target capacity of 30GW. In addition, the NEA aggressively hopes to see the capacity of solar power hit the new target of 10GW–20GW by 2020, 5.5–11 times the current target of 1.8GW. It is estimated that the total investment needed to reach these new targets will be over 3 trillion RMB Yuan, or $439 billion (USD).

OUTLOOK FOR EMERGING MARKETS: A GREEN, CLEAN INDUSTRIAL REVOLUTION?

As the developed and emerging world strives to evolve into a greener, cleaner, and more efficient place, energy infrastructure's importance and relevance will no doubt continue to grow. Economic conditions will also play a role in the choices made by governments. Depending on the country or technology, these may be complementary factors or conflicting. However, as the private sector's role increases, and new technologies become more cost efficient, green energy may prove to be a high growth sector of the global economy.

Emerging market economies, however, have clear risks to investors, and energy infrastructure is not immune to this fact. A prolonged global recession, for example, could prove more damaging to a relatively fragile emerging country than to a developed one, leading to renewed instability or retrenchment. Thus, predicting investment success in emerging markets relative to risk is more difficult than in a developed country with stable and mature legal, regulatory, financial market and political establishments. That said, the durable nature of infrastructure assets and the demand profile for energy and power in high-growth, high-population economies such as India and China make this asset class potentially attractive on a risk-reward basis than other financial market investments that are more economically sensitive. We believe that a strong partnership between governments and private sector investment is a vital component of the long-term success of energy infrastructure in emerging markets.

The demand for infrastructure investment is growing around the world not only because of demographic and macroeconomic trends, but also because of the necessity and burden of maintaining existing and aging infrastructure. Governments in developed and developing countries alike face similar challenges in providing and maintaining the infrastructure required for sustainable growth. Private equity funds can provide both the infusion of capital needed by these governments and access for investors to an attractive opportunity in a rapidly growing global necessity.

CONTRIBUTOR DISCLAIMER

All material presented is compiled from sources believed to be reliable and current, but accuracy cannot be guaranteed.

This is not to be construed as an offer to buy or sell any financial instruments and should not be relied upon as the sole factor in an investment-making decision. As with all investments, there are associated inherent risks. Please obtain and review all financial material carefully before investing. This does not constitute a recommendation of the suitability of any investment strategy for a particular investor. The opinions expressed herein are based on current market conditions and are subject to change without notice.

ENDNOTES

1. RREEF Research, "Asian Infrastructure Markets: Exploring Current Trends in a Changing Market," November, 2006. www.rreef.com.
2. World Bank, "Connecting East Asia; New Framework for Infrastructure," 2005.
3. RREEF Research, "Asian Infrastructure Markets: Exploring Current Trends in a Changing Market."
4. Ibid.
5. Ibid.
6. Ibid.
7. CEIC Data, 2008. www.ceicdata.com; Invesco Private Capital, "The Opportunity in Global Infrastructure Investment," July, 2008.
8. RREEF Research, "Asian Infrastructure Markets: Exploring Current Trends in a Changing Market."
9. "Strengthening Public Infrastructure Investment Policy in China: Strategic Options for Central, Provincial and Local Governments," report issued by the Asian Development Bank and the Ministry of Finance, China, June 2002, 16. www.adb.org/Documents/Reports/PRC-Public-Infrastructure/prelims.pdf.
10. Data released from China's Chinese Wind Energy Association, December, 2008. www.cwea.org.cn (Chinese government agency web site).

CHAPTER 4

Infrastructure Investing in the Electric Power Sector

Douglas W. Kimmelman
Senior Partner, Energy Capital Partners

Electricity is the backbone of any mature economic system, and the capital requirements to maintain its reliable service are both large and continuous. A developed society cannot function without electricity, and its importance grows as usage expands into such areas as digital applications, mobile computing, and electric vehicles. Approximately 80 percent of electricity usage is for residential or commercial activities, largely insulating usage trends from the level of economic activity and more correlating usage with population trends. Surprising to most, electricity is the most capital intensive industry in North America and has evolved into a traded commodity market with revenues in excess of that of the oil and gas industries. The industrywide asset base totals over $750 billion, with annual revenues of over $350 billion and includes over 5000 individual power facilities and 160,000 miles of transmission lines.

Complementing these basic needs for electricity is a need to replace and upgrade an aged asset base that is in many cases over 40 years old, a need to comply with heightened environmental mandates in the areas of CO^2, mercury, sulfur dioxide, and nitrous oxide, and a requirement to meet renewable power mandates that have spread across 30 states.

The transmission grid is antiquated. It was not built for a deregulated marketplace that has evolved in the past decade and certainly was not built with the notion of remote wind and solar renewable power needing to be connected to distant population centers.

All of these factors are exacerbated by the fragmented nature of the electric power industry. There are over 3,000 providers of utility services and owners of power assets in the United States. No one entity has even a 5 percent market share of power generation. There are no dominant power players with large liquid balance sheets that can meet all of their own capital needs. Unlike Europe that generally has a few strong and large utilities covering the entire country (think EDF, E.ON or Endesa), the United States is saturated with a diverse group of providers. California, for example, has dozens of electricity providers including Southern California Edison, Pacific Gas & Electric, San Diego Gas & Electric, Los Angeles Department of Water & Power, Imperial Irrigation District and city-owned systems such as Anaheim, Burbank, and Riverside and municipal systems such as the Sacramento Municipal Utility System. Add to that dozens of independent owners of assets such as Dynegy, NRG, and Calpine and you can imagine the challenge of figuring out who can and will own and build the massive volume of power infrastructure assets needed to maintain system reliability and economic growth while meeting the various public policy environmental mandates coming rapidly from both federal and state legislative initiatives.

STRUCTURAL ELEMENTS OF THE POWER SECTOR

Delivering reliable electric power to homes, businesses, and factories is a far more complex undertaking than most people realize when they flip on the light switch. Most important, electricity is the only commodity that cannot be stored on a commercially meaningful scale. You cannot put it into a bucket for use when you need it—it is a business without a real-time inventory—you have to produce it in real time to coincide exactly with an unpredictable level of demand. Demand fluctuates widely throughout the day and the year with weather variability, low nighttime usage, and seasonal demand trends. Supply also is not constant as plants go out of service routinely for both scheduled and unscheduled maintenance outages. Most power facilities sit largely idle at night and require a massive network of back-up facilities at peak demand points throughout the day and the year. Some power plants run no more than 25 hours a year and are in service only for perhaps a peak air conditioning day in August. Supply and demand must be instantaneously matched or the grid will fail, causing widespread loss of service (blackouts). As a result, the system must be built with sufficient capacity and redundancy to assure a high degree of reliability at the moment of peak demand during the year.

The regulated utility used to exist in a vertically integrated model where one company owned all of the three major functions of an electric utility—generation, transmission, and distribution. It could do its own system planning and all of its costs of capital, fuel, and operations and maintenance (O&M) expenses were passed through to customers in a state-by-state regulated rate of return process. This regulated structure largely has been replaced in most regions of the country with a deregulated model that separates the still-regulated local distribution of power (a natural monopoly) from the newly deregulated production function. The theory is that the local distribution company or customer should not have to buy electricity from one captive generator, but should be able to shop the market for the lowest priced alternative. This state-by-state movement toward deregulation gave rise to a new industry, the independent power producer sector (IPPs). These IPPs have grown rapidly in size and number over the past 15 years. They acquired many of the power plants in the United States that were required to be divested by the incumbent deregulating utilities and became the dominant builder of new facilities.

A few of the IPPs are publicly traded, many are private, independent entities controlled by private pools of capital, some are nonregulated subsidiaries of otherwise regulated utilities and others are subsidiaries of large energy companies, equipment suppliers, financial institutions or foreign utilities.

PRICING MODELS

Most think of the electric power industry as one with capped returns set at low levels by state regulators. That structure remains true for roughly 35 percent of the asset base of the industry, the regulated local distribution function, but new pricing models largely have evolved for the remainder—the generation and transmission sectors.

Generation, or the production of electricity, comprises over 50 percent of the asset base of the industry and over 50 percent of your electric bill. While some utilities remain integrated and regulated as to the rates charged, most have separated from the generation function (through divestiture or financial separation) and buy their electricity needs on the open market. The regulated distribution utility shops the market for electricity in meeting its number one priority of maintaining system reliability. Utilities in states like California and New York own virtually no power plants and must buy their power from others. An open market system has evolved where utilities buy their needs both on a spot market hour-to-hour basis as well as through long-term contracts through negotiated and competitive processes. The contracts can be for the physical delivery of electricity, referred to as *energy payments*, or can be for capacity, basically an insurance premium payment to have a power station available for peak system needs. Utilities will transact with other utilities, financial commodity intermediaries, and independent owners of power facilities for their needs.

The distribution function that has remained rate regulated comprises about 35 percent of industry assets and will have the rate it charges customers set as both a pass-through of operating expenses and purchased power costs as well as through an allowed equity return on the equity component of capital expended to build and maintain the physical operating distribution network. A growing rate base will grow the earnings power of the distribution utility; however, no earnings are generated through funds spent to procure power from third-party generators.

Transmission, or the long haul movement of electricity from central station power stations to in-city distribution systems, comprises the remaining 15 percent of industry assets and increasingly serves a critical role in interconnecting markets to accomplish the goals of deregulation. The electrification of the United States in the past 100 years was largely done on a regional basis as directed by federal legislation (the Public Utility Holding Company Act of 1935), and, therefore, the existing transmission system has been ill-equipped to move power across neighboring markets. The 2005 Energy Bill put forth an incentive rate structure set by the Federal Energy Regulatory Commission to encourage new building of transmission to enable the interconnection of markets and the hook-up of renewable power projects that are most often located in remote locations (especially solar and wind). To attract the needed capital investment, the rate mechanism provides an attractive 13 percent to 14 percent after-tax return on equity on an assumed 50 percent debt and 50 percent equity capital structure and explicitly allows for back leverage and the potential to achieve pretax levered returns in excess of 20 percent. While potential returns are attractive, transmission lines traversing several hundreds of miles are often faced with many permitting and rights-of-way challenges and can often take years of preconstruction development activity in order to move forward.

THE STORAGE CONUNDRUM

Electricity might have been a simple business to design and manage if it had a workable inventory system like virtually every other business in the world. The physical nature of electricity does not allow it to be stored in large quantities in the form of electricity. Power must be produced in real time to match customer demand. Due to the uncertainties of weather and demand trends, a significant overbuild of the system must occur. The required back-up or excess reserve margin has the effect of dramatically adding to the cost of electricity and must also drive pricing models with capacity payments to encourage the building and ownership of facilities that will run only infrequently at extreme peak demand periods.

Significant investment, especially in the venture arena, is focused on solving the storage issue. Battery technologies have promise, but remain only at small scale. Large hydro-pumped storage systems where excess, low-cost nighttime electricity is used to pump water uphill to fill a reservoir that can be released to produce hydro power at peak demand daytime periods are few and far between and are extremely expensive to build and hard to permit. Areas where wind is a nighttime resource with little value are being evaluated as a complement to a pumped storage system where the wind power could be used as the low-cost electricity source for pumping requirements. Compressed air projects where air can be pressurized into an underground reservoir using cheap nighttime electricity and then reversed to turn a turbine during peak demand periods are also under evaluation. The real answer to storage may lie in the use of excess nighttime power. Nuclear and coal facilities that combine for 70 percent of our power needs in the United States cannot be cycled off and on quickly as they can take days to restart. These plants cannot be totally shut off at night when demand for electricity drops. Therefore, much of the current focus is on how to efficiently use this low-cost excess nighttime power. Electric vehicles are central to this thinking as perhaps the excess power can be used to charge electric vehicles at night for use during the next business day.

INVESTMENT FUNDAMENTALS

The most basic decisions to be evaluated in investing in the power sector fall in several categories:

- Regulated versus unregulated assets
- Contracted or hedged versus merchant or unhedged ownership positions
- Existing operating assets versus new build development projects
- Active ownership with execution of value creation plan versus passive ownership of bond-like streams
- Technology/venture stage investing versus real asset ownership
- Prioritizing investment objectives of income generation, capital gains, investment holding period, and inflation hedging

Regulated Versus Unregulated Assets

The regulated versus unregulated decision rests in one's view of the con-structiveness of the regulatory environment. Will the elected/appointed state regulators be constructive in allowing equity to earn premium returns should performance be positive or will they channel any excess earnings over allowed levels into rate reductions? Will the regulator welcome outside private capital in owning an asset deemed to be a public good or will they block the takeover or at least take multiple years of hearings prior to approval and attach many conditions to their approval? The history of mergers and takeovers in the utility sector is quite checkered. Many transactions have been blocked by regulators or transactions have been terminated due to excessive rate concession demands. Hostile takeovers have rarely succeeded as the incumbent utility generally has had a solid backing of all of its local constituents.

Unregulated generating assets comprise the single largest asset component of the industry, yet it can carry a high degree of risk as pricing is fully set by market mechanisms. Can the investor[s] successfully time the commodity price cycle in owning unregulated generation or can the investor[s] put in place an effective contracting and hedging program? Leverage may be more widely available for regulated assets while unregulated assets may be more exposed to the cycles of capital availability in the credit markets.

Hedging Decision

The decision to contract or hedge the output of a power facility relates largely to one's desire to speculate in commodity prices as well as to the availability of attractive off-take terms and the relative point in the commodity price cycle. Most power stations have dual commodity price risk in that they generally buy coal or natural gas and convert it into electricity. Commodity input and output exposures must be managed and one must consider the relative efficiency or heat rate of the plant in question. Older, inefficient, or higher heat rate plants may be cheap to buy, but may only be called upon to run in the most extreme of demand situations. Other valuation factors include the possible existence in some markets of additional revenues from capacity payments and ancillary services, the potential for competing new build facilities as well as the potential for the retirement of existing plants.

Contracts for the output of a power facility sold back to a utility may limit the upside should commodity markets tighten, but can provide several meaningful downside benefits. Power purchase arrangements with utilities often have a term of from 5 years to 30 years, they generally provide for a pass-through of fuel costs, and historically have been readily financable in even the most challenging of credit markets. Default risk is all but nonexistent as the sanctity of contract and the need for reliable power purchases have protected power purchase arrangements even in the case of a bankruptcy of the underlying utility. A deep list of purchasers generally has existed throughout market cycles for long-dated contracted assets especially from public energy companies seeking earnings and cash flow as well as from late-stage infrastructure funds looking for long-dated assets with distributable income.

Buy Versus Build Decision

Working through the development process to build a new energy asset requires a different and more complex set of skills than buying and managing an existing operating asset. Greenfield development involves a somewhat uncertain and long road of obtaining local permits to build a new facility, while advance-stage development strategies often allow one to buy into a development project once it has cleared early-stage permitting and rights-of-way challenges. Beyond Greenfield-permitting challenges that generally are led by complexities in receiving air and water permits, a developer must decide if he will be endeavoring to contract the output of the facility, if a fixed price turn-key construction contract will be put in place, and if a construction financing loan can be obtained. The more structured the project with locked-in revenue and cost variables, the more aggressive the financing package that generally can be put in place. A merchant, uncontracted new build project with uncertain construction costs is not one that is likely to attract very much, if any, debt financing.

The buy-versus-build decision also is influenced greatly by relative valuations. A new build project often can produce cash flows at a much lower valuation or cost to build than buying an existing asset if it is solving a challenge for a utility or exists in a tight supply/demand location where an existing asset is not located. Higher cash flow margins may be available if a utility has enough need for a location-specific project, or perhaps is under a regulatory mandate to add a certain type of power, especially renewable power. A contract or forward sale of power at attractive margins at times can be achieved on a new build asset if the location is right and if existing assets are unable to fill the location-specific need.

Existing asset valuations have experienced a volatile recent historic trend that has been driven by great swings in commodity prices, financing availability, and the relative strength of buyers and sellers. At times, buying an existing asset below replacement cost can provide for a long-term attractive upside should commodity prices firm and the asset remains unhedged. However, the buying below replacement cost paradigm also can be a precursor to bankruptcy should commodity prices not recover and revenues from spot energy sales remain insufficient to cover fixed costs in areas such as debt service, maintenance, property taxes, insurance, and so on. The bankruptcies of Calpine and Mirant in recent years and the current weak stock prices of the publicly traded merchant power companies are good examples of the significant downside risks inherent in an unhedged operating power facility. Extended cycles of operating facilities rarely turning on to generate any electricity have been commonplace in periods of high gas and coal input prices relative to a soft market for the electricity output.

Lastly, the timing of cash flows during the development phase of a project can be inconsistent with the specific requirements of certain asset owners. Owners such as infrastructure funds or public companies often only will want to hold assets that produce current income and cash flows consistent with their distribution or dividend payment goals. This factor historically has reduced the competition for development stage projects meaningfully. Private equity owners who are more focused on long-term capital appreciation goals increasingly have been moving into development projects. Limited Partners (LPs) in these funds have come to understand the deferred capital call nature of a new build project versus an operating project acquisition. The typical five-year commitment period for a private equity fund must be monitored closely when pursuing multiyear development projects.

Active Versus Passive Ownership

Many investors in power assets choose to allow others to do the new build development work and to manage the operations of the facilities. These investors are looking merely to acquire a largely fixed bondlike cash flow stream that is generated from the facility and often are minority interest owners. The returns available for this stage of ownership generally are at the low end of sector returns, perhaps in the mid-teens area. Historically, premium returns have been available for those who have successfully brought development projects on line and who have been able to add value to plant cash flows through active management. Examples of active value-creation strategies in addition to successful development include contract restructurings, asset expansions, optimizing fuel supply arrangements, hedging strategies, maintenance practices, workforce efficiencies, and optimizing property tax and insurance obligations.

Venture Stage Investing Versus Real Asset Ownership

Much attention recently has been devoted to clean-tech investments that are being pursued in several areas:

- Renewable power efficiencies
- Electricity storage applications

- Electric vehicles and improved battery technologies
- Smart grid and energy efficiency platforms
- Clean coal innovations

These investments are early stage by nature and require relatively modest capital during the product development stage with greatly accelerating capital needs as a product is built out at scale for commercial applications. Small projects are of little impactful value in an electric utility industry of massive scale. Investing in a new concept can reap great rewards if commercial acceptance is achieved; however, the large equity requirements of a commercial buildout are not necessarily the mandate of a venture investor.

An important transition generally will be required to bring in more traditional private capital in scale to lead the funding of a late-stage buildout of a large solar field, for example. A major challenge for a venture investor in such an example where perhaps a new higher efficiency solar application has been developed will be to attract funding for the commercial deployment of such a new technology. Infrastructure investors generally prefer to back projects using proven technologies; bridging the funding gap for that first generation of utility scale projects between venture and infrastructure investors remains a challenge, and therefore, the lines between venture and real asset ownership in the power sector have become a bit blurred.

Prioritizing Investment Objectives

Investors each have their own specific objectives in terms of risk reward parameters, investment holding periods, and desire for income generation or long-term capital gains. These objectives or investment mandates can influence greatly the stage and structure of how one invests in the power sector. The 40-year or so life of a power project can be characterized by a higher risk reward period during development with negative cash flows evolving into a longer term remaining period of general stability during operations with stable positive cash flows assuming a hedged or contracted model. Not all investors are comfortable in each of these stages.

Is the strategy one to maximize returns over a five-year period with a focus on capital gains or is it more of a late-stage plan to generate cash distributions through the operating life of the facility?

Real assets inherently provide a hedge against inflation as returns are influenced greatly by terminal values that correlate highly to the level of commodity prices and inflation in the economy. One needs to decide if they want to concentrate this hedge by allowing a power project to not lock in its revenue structure and further float as commodity prices fluctuate.

INVESTMENT RISKS

Electricity has been viewed historically as a flight to quality investment sector with downside protection coming from a regulatory compact. This remains largely true in the still regulated distribution sector; however, deregulation has introduced multiple risks to the ownership of nonregulated power assets.

The largest risks center on commodity pricing exposure especially when it is magnified by an often significant chunk of leverage in the capital structure of an asset. Investors who choose to float on their fuel purchases and their power sales are subject to an extreme variability of cash flow performance and ability to amortize debt on the project. Timing the entry and exit of an asset within commodity cycles is therefore a critical factor driving cash-flow generation on a merchant or unhedged asset. Revenue variability also can be impacted in markets where capacity payments are made to installed generation and where these capacity payments vary by market-setting processes.

Operating risks cannot be ignored in the power sector—the manufacturing of electricity is a mechanical and labor-intensive undertaking. Extended and unscheduled outages do occur. A damaged turbine blade, a tube leak, or a blown transformer are all examples of equipment failures that could shut down a facility for an extended period, putting cash-flow generation at risk. Equipment warranties generally are available for the first year or two of operations and business outage insurance generally is available for outages that go beyond 30 or 60 days.

Safe, reliable, and environmentally compliant operations are core to any power operating system. Every power facility has a detailed air and water permit that must be complied with on a daily basis—self-monitoring any violations and promptly reporting them is core to a culture of operational excellence.

Fuel availability is another area of potential uncertainty. A gas-fired power plant generally does not face this risk as it will have dedicated pipeline access to gas supplies. Coal-fired plants generally will sign long-term coal supply and rail or barge transportation arrangements; however, the logistics of always insuring ample coal supply inventories on site can be complex and sometimes uncertain.

The availability of leverage is not as great a risk in the power sector as often experienced in other more cyclical industries or in leveraged buyout (LBO) business models. As previously discussed, contracted business models generally have financed quite successfully through credit cycles versus more challenges for merchant facilities. Utilities often see better debt availability in tougher credit markets since they are viewed as a very safe credit risk; note over $35 billion of long-term debt being issued for U.S. utilities in the

October 2008 to July 2009 time frame, notwithstanding the severity of the credit crunch during this period.

Development projects carry their own unique risks of permitting and on time and budget construction, which is often mitigated by fixed construction contracts. Lastly, the value that buyers and sellers attribute to power assets has fluctuated greatly throughout market cycles. We have seen an earnings before interest, taxes, depreciation and amortization (EBITDA) multiple value range of perhaps 5 times to 12 times over the past 15 years and values have cycled through this full range three times during the period. Timing one's purchase and sale within this cycle will have a meaningful impact on achieved returns.

Renewable Power Opportunities

Thirty states are now requiring utilities to generate from 10 percent to 30 percent of their power from renewable resources. Since most of these utilities are no longer in the power generation business or do not have the balance sheets to pursue large build capital projects, they have generally offered 25- to 30-year contracts to purchase renewable power from projects developed by independent third parties.

These contracts are awarded based on several factors:

- Price of power delivered and timing of delivery
- Location of the project and degree of transmission hook-up challenges
- Reliability and track record of technology
- Credibility of the developer and source of funding
- Project permitting challenges
- Project progress on land and equipment procurement

Wind and solar have dominated new utility scale renewable projects in the past few years. Both are generally remotely located, and transmission availability has been the major impediment to growth. The federal government is trying aggressively to facilitate the development of these types of projects through the offering of 30 percent investment tax credits as well as a pool of $60 billion in loan guarantees for the construction of new renewable projects. California utilities collectively are signing several thousand megawatts of 25-year renewable contracts each year. A typical 100 megawatt solar contract could produce over $1 billion in life of contract revenues. A land rush and transmission access rush clearly has been underway by multiple developers in efforts to secure these long-dated, stable, and financeable revenue streams from quite creditworthy counterparties.

While the unprecedented availability of long-term contracts is real, renewable development is not without challenges. Land in close proximity to transmission access that has minimal local permitting challenges is becoming more competitive to secure. Equipment with a proven track record that can be financed and carries a creditworthy performance guarantee is a prerequisite. Many of the new technologies being developed are not yet ready to meet this standard, so equipment purchases are becoming concentrated among the incumbent suppliers such as GE and Vestas in wind and First Solar and SunPower in photovoltaics (PV) solar. The process to apply for government programs for tax credits and loan guarantees is still evolving so some delays on the financing front remain.

Pending federal legislation to institute a cap and trade system to reduce CO_2 emissions as well as a provision for a national renewable power standard could further stimulate renewable activity in the United States.

Future of Conventional Power Sources

Currently, power production in the United States is sourced from coal (50 percent), natural gas (20 percent), nuclear (20 percent), hydro (6 percent), and other largely renewable sources (4 percent).

A nuclear renaissance in the United States has been much discussed and many utilities are readying plans to build the next generation of nuclear plants. Currently, there are 104 operating nuclear facilities in the United States, and, while many countries generate a greater percentage of their power from nuclear than the United States, the U.S. nuclear industry continues to produce the largest number of megawatt hours in the world. The challenges for a new build cycle rest predominantly in an inability to budget for an accurate cost of construction as a standard new plant design has not yet been approved by the Nuclear Regulatory Commission (NRC) and no engineering and construction firm has yet come forward to guarantee the cost of construction for a new facility.

Coal is the predominant available fuel source in the United States and its availability and high BTU content has led over the past several decades to coal becoming the dominant source of power generation in the United States. However, global warming concerns have halted most new coal development plans as the sector is facing uncertain new CO_2 emission caps and regulations. This pause in coal development has squarely shifted new development focus to gas-fired power generation sources, especially with gas currently selling for historically low prices.

Hydro power is an important low-cost resource in many U.S. regions, especially the Pacific Northwest. Generally, most rivers worthy of hydro generation have been dammed to their maximum capacity, and new hydro developments are quite the exception.

Many experts are focused on nuclear as an effective source of power that effectively combats the greenhouse gas issue, but more work is needed on developing effective storage plans for nuclear waste. Coal's future may rest on the effectiveness of coal gasification technologies to effectively separate and store the CO_2 emitted from burning coal. Gas plants currently are flourishing in this low-gas-price environment, but would face greater challenges should we see an upward shift in commodity prices. Renewable plants may be the answer in moving away from conventional sources, but without subsidies, most renewable sources of power remain at a cost of nearly double a fossil option.

CONCLUSION

The movement away from the regulated and integrated utility model over the past 15 years has generated many investment opportunities in the electric power sector, which remains the most capital intensive sector in the nation. Investment performance by a new class of nonutility owners generally has been good with the most recurring disappointments occurring by those who aggressively pursued leveraged investments into assets with open-ended commodity price risks. For those that have had a bias to contracting and hedging these price exposures, performance has been consistently solid.

Asset turnover continues at a rapid pace as more independent and foreign owners enter the sector and as more utilities gravitate away from generation and concentrate their focus on the regulated side of the business.

The development of new assets continues to be an essential component of the sector and continues to drive the heaviest concentration of new investment capital. New assets are needed to replace aging infrastructure, to keep up with population shifts across the nation, and to comply with a desire for new cleaner and greener sources of electricity. Infrastructure funds, private equity funds, foreign utilities, equipment suppliers, and financial firms continue to invest heavily in the sector in efforts to achieve high levels of stable returns.

CHAPTER 5

Water and Wastewater Infrastructure

Michael D. Underhill
Founder, Capital Innovations LLC

Ian Savage Elliott

In order to understand the role that infrastructure can play in water utilities, it is first necessary to examine the water crisis in detail. The global water crisis is one of the most underreported challenges facing the international community. The near-term future looks challenging, and the long-term forecast potentially disastrous to human health, agriculture, and industry. While this picture has grim implications for people, it does indicate the need for substantially new infrastructure investment.

There are two basic methods of investing in water infrastructure: through the privatization of municipal water systems and via water conservation technologies. Privatization offers ample opportunity for continued growth of the private and public water infrastructure markets; however, these opportunities must be carefully monitored to ensure that private sector profit requirements, government expectations, and public opinion are all accounted for. Desalination and wastewater treatment are two water conservation techniques that will also contribute in combating water shortage, as these technologies expand their market share and geographic reach. Overall, the water crisis demands so much capital for the prevention of disease, death, and economic hardship, that private and public investment in water infrastructure is necessary to help improve access and relieve the budget strain on governments. This will be done through privatization of water systems and technological advancement of water technologies. However, there is a public resistance in certain areas to private sector involvement in the water sector, and to paying higher level charges for the collection, treatment, and distribution of potable water.

This chapter begins with an examination of water usage and the impending water shortage facing the globe. It then assesses the greatest challenges to maintaining supply and the insufficiencies of current water storage mechanisms. The second half of the chapter discusses the future of privatization in the municipal water and services and technologies sector, highlighting some key features that will drive successful privatization attempts moving forward. Finally, the last section details two other water technology solutions that will be expanding as a result of the water crisis.

WATER STRESS

Although water is arguably the most important resource on the planet, many people are unaware of how it is actually allocated. The vast majority of global water withdrawals (about 74 percent) are for agricultural use, compared with domestic purposes (8 percent) and industry (18 percent).[1] The damage of a water shortage is incredibly widespread. More than 2.8 billion people in 48 countries will face water stress or scarcity conditions by 2025.[2] By the middle of this century, 7 billion people in 60 countries could be facing water scarcity.[3] All three areas (agriculture, domestic, and industry) are currently suffering, and stand to deteriorate rapidly over the coming years, as outlined in the two sections that follow. Further, agricultural demand has been affected by the move, in some areas of the world, into crops that are more water intensive in their cultivation (rice is an example). Patterns of agriculture may need to change to accommodate a limited supply of water.

Access to Clean Water

On the human health side, access to clean drinking water is already an issue in much of the developing world. Seven million people die annually because of water-borne diseases, of which 2.2 million are under 5 years of age.[4] The World Economic Forum (WEF) estimates that from 1900 to 2000, water withdrawal expanded at a rate more than double that of population increase—ninefold and fourfold, respectively. According to the United Nations (2008), there are 1.8 billion people without access to clean drinking water.[5] The Organization for Economic Co-operation and Development (OECD) estimates that 2.8 billion people live in areas of high water stress, and predicts this number will rise rapidly, reaching almost 4 billion by the year 2030. The risk of insufficient water expands far beyond the human health problem, with drastic implications for both agriculture and industry.

However, many of the human health problems are experienced in developing countries, where the ability to pay for improvements in water collection, treatment, and distribution is limited.

Agriculture

In agriculture and industry, water is a key determinant of a country's output and trading power. As previously stated, agriculture dominates water usage. Furthermore, deficiencies in the traditional water withdrawal process in most water-scarce countries means that of the water withdrawn, roughly 50 percent is evaporated or lost in the removal process.[6] In the near future, agriculture stands to become a larger issue, as the same study estimates that 55 percent of the world's population will be dependent on food imports by 2030 as a result of insufficient domestic water. By importing cereal, meat, and other food products, countries can reduce their direct agricultural water use. Currently, three of the top-10 food exporters are water-scarce countries, and three of the top-10 food importers water-rich countries. If the current water scarcity problem remains unaddressed, these current import and export practices are unsustainable. It will be difficult to change the list of net exporters and net importers in the agricultural industry. Agricultural trade, which has declined over the past 20 years as a result of food price volatility and more competitive, dynamic global trading markets, is going to need to improve and increase in order to engulf the massive demand created by the water crisis. With more people reliant on food imports, the water-rich, water-poor divide will become a key differentiator in global agricultural production and pricing. However, part of this imbalance may be dealt with through the reallocation of agricultural resources globally. For instance, as income per head in Asia increased over the past 20 years, the demand for water-intensive vegetables has increased. This lucrative market has led to farmers in some water-deficient areas of Australia to step into this market. However, continued droughts in Australia are choking off the industry there, and may lead to a move back to more traditional, less water intensive, cultivation.

Industry

Similar to agriculture, industrial practices are widely water dependent. A 2006 study by the nonprofit WaterWise found that the daily usage of water in the United Kingdom is 3,400 litres daily, 65 percent was embedded in food, 30 percent embedded in industrial goods, 4.2 percent embedded in domestic goods, and 0.2 percent embedded in drinking water.[7] The water used to produce goods for export is known as *virtual water*. Currently, most trade isn't based on virtual water, but as scarcity increases, industry, like agriculture, will be divided, with water-heavy countries standing to benefit from the savings accrued via virtual water.[8] Moving forward, water-scarce nations must decide how best to allocate their renewable water resources. Currently, according to the World Economic Forum (2009), countries have a 40 percent agricultural threshold for renewable water resources, after which point a developing nation will be unable to adequately allocate water to both the agricultural sector, and the urban municipal and industrial sectors.[9] By 2030, WEF estimates that all of South Asia will reach the 40 percent threshold whilst the Middle East and North Africa region will have hit 58 percent.[10]

Current industrial and agricultural processes are unable to withstand current water usage. With increased water scarcity and continual water usage practices, countries will be forced to decide between their growing economy and feeding their citizens. Furthermore, both processes will have to increase their overall output (in terms of trading volumes), led by nations heavy with virtual water, unless current water practices are remedied. The evolution of this decision-making process will be instructive, particularly as, on a stand-alone basis, industry tends to be more able to pay for its own water extraction and wastewater treatment—certainly more so than agriculture.

THE INADEQUACY AND OVERUSE OF CURRENT WATER STORAGE MECHANISMS

Before examining the role of the private sector and water infrastructure in the future, it is necessary to understand current water storage and transfer mechanisms available in response to the water scarcity crisis. This section outlines two of the largest problems in water supply management: the unsustainability of dams and the current overexploitation of groundwater. These two processes, which represent the bulk of the current water supply management mechanisms, are functioning inadequately, providing short-term benefit at the expense of long-term environmental destruction and water devastation.

Dams

Dams are one of the primary mechanisms employed for controlling water supply; they also can be used to regulate water flow, control flooding, or for hydroelectric power. In the second half of the 20th century, the World Bank spent $75 billion on building large dams in 92 countries. Dams are now present on the 20 largest rivers in the world, as well as the 8 with the most biological diversity—the Amazon, Orinco, Ganges, Brahmaputra, Zambezi, Amut, Yenisei, and Indus.[11] The largest river without a dam is the Yukon in northern Canada—the 22nd largest river in the world. For the purposes of this study, we examine their usage and effects on water supply and quality, leaving out the power-generating aspect of the argument. Bear in mind, most dams are not power suppliers—only approximately 3 percent of the 80,000 dams in the United States provide hydroelectric power generation.[12] The number of large dams has increased approximately 900 percent during the latter half of the 20th century, as dams became the catchall solution to water shortage. While dams achieved their goal in the short term by making water available to those who need it, they also create various side effects, including the interruption of river flow, destruction of vegetation and animal life, and disruption of nutrient flows.[13]

Dams are incredibly destructive to rivers, vegetation life, animals, and people. Sediment naturally accumulates within rivers; however, it is equally dispersed via the flow of water. Patrick McCully's *Silenced Rivers: The Ecology and Politics of Large Dams* provides an explanation of how high the sediment levels can climb: "The proportion of a river's total sediment load captured by a dam—known as its 'trap efficiency'—approaches 100 per cent for many projects, especially those with large reservoirs" (p. 349). Sediment accumulation causes dams to lose their ability to store useable water, effectively rendering the dam useless. There has been little progression in sedimentation research, with the problem still widely effecting dams at different rates. Sedimentation, as well as rising water levels, impact animal spawning beds and create unnatural habitat changes, the most publicly noted damages being to the spawning cycle of the salmon.[14] Dams have desiccated wetlands, damaging the world's irrigated land with salt and waterlogging. Similarly, the effects of dams on forced relocation (due to flooding or otherwise) are staggering—at least 80 million people worldwide have lost their home and lands.[15] Rather than fixing the water storage problem, these dams temporarily provide adequate water storage at the expense of damaging long-term water supply and destroying plant, animal, and human livelihood.

Groundwater Extraction

Groundwater is the result of rainfall soaked into the ground, eventually trickling downward and saturating rocks below ground level. At this point, the water will flow into a point of discharge, mainly a body of water such as a lake or river. The permeable formations that contain groundwater are known as *aquifers*. Unlike artificial, man-made dams, groundwater is a natural occurrence. Groundwater can be accessed in a number of ways, including springs, wells, and electrically driven pumps. It is the first resort to water scarcity, representing 50 percent of all drinking water.[16] However, excessive groundwater usage can lead to a host of issues, mainly the depletion of aquifers. If water is overpumped from aquifers, the water level in the aquifer falls. This increases the cost of pumping water, and also threatens the body of water that the aquifer flows into. Overextraction of groundwater can also lead to increased salinity or inundation of the freshwater table by saline water. This has disastrously occurred in some low lying countries in Asia, rending previously fertile land unusable.

While groundwater represents a sustainable solution, it is currently being vastly overused. According to the United Nations, the aquifers that are being pumped are outpacing the natural replacement rate, especially in regions with low recharge rate.[17] In the World Water Development Report, the UN points out that around 20 percent of the total water used globally is from groundwater sources, but this number has been rapidly rising. Groundwater is not monitored in most nations, so understanding groundwater level abuse or comparing nations is impossible. Inadequate provisions from cities and states have caused a rise in unregulated personal and private usage of groundwater. According to the OECD,[18] groundwater withdrawals rose fivefold during the 20th century, including an increase of 11 percent since 1980 in the OECD nations. Nations such as Mexico, China, Peru, Zambia, and India have cities heavily reliant on groundwater. Clearly, it is not a problem unique to any one geography or economy.

Other Examples

While groundwater and dams represent two dramatic examples of water supply abuse, they are by no means the only transgressors. In the United States, only one-quarter of the water used historically comes from groundwater; however water pollution and shortage will also threaten the U.S. water supplies. In terms of U.S.-based shortages, California's water crisis and deteriorating levees threaten to destroy the state's main drinking and agriculture water supply within the next 30 years. Statewide storage capacity, if the levees are sustained, will cost taxpayers an estimated $1.6 billion per year through 2020 to support California's water crisis management.[19]

Likewise, water transfers such as the South-North Water Transfer in China, which sends water from the Yangtze River to the Yellow River, has been unsuccessful and environmentally hazardous. The project was supposed to manifest Mao Zedong's vision of "lending water from the south to the north," ameliorating Beijing and North China's water crisis. It has required a massive commitment from the South: 50,000 residents of Habei were forced to relocate after water transfers from their region to Beijing. Habei residents also complained of reduced agricultural revenues as a result of limited access to the river, their main irrigation tool. The environmental risks of this project (or any project moving millions of gallons of water via interbasin transfer) include a loss of soil fertility, land erosion, and changed species migratory patterns. The transfer has generally failed to solve the problem: Beijing is still abusing groundwater resources. A 2008 *Economist* magazine article cites a study by Probe International, which highlights some striking estimates: Beijing's reservoirs are down to one-tenth of their capacity, two-thirds of their water supply relies on groundwater, and the water table is dropping by approximately one meter a year.[20] Case studies of China, India, and Australia reveal that governments have had little success in alternative solutions to water management when faced with a reduction of rainfall.

WATER TREATMENT AND THE INFRASTRUCTURE OPPORTUNITY: PART OF THE SOLUTION

The massive shortage between supply and demand lends itself to the injection of private capital and competence. The gap between water reserves and usage continues to grow, and the mechanisms of treating water are currently not large enough to maintain supply. The private sector can also prioritize investment decisions to get the best value for its customers. Furthermore, without properly mobilized political support, there is no way to change the habits of industry, agriculture, and the everyday citizen. As usage increases and supply diminishes, the viability of, and the support for privatization rises. Privatization has led to increased water access, decreased disease, and in many cases lower prices. It still remains a challenging endeavor however, requiring substantial public support, a strong regulatory power, and a commitment to long-term success regardless of short-term economic fluctuations.

The next section examines both the public and private opportunity for infrastructure investment. The privatization of urban water and wastewater services will continue to grow, as both OECD and developing nations are unable to deliver effective urban water solutions and continue to invest in water treatment facilities on their own accord. Similarly, the opportunity for water infrastructure companies that can recycle or conserve water reserves will be much needed in the areas of desalination and wastewater treatment.

Privatization of Urban Water and Wastewater Services

Improving water delivery, minimizing costs, and increasing effectiveness of water recycling necessitates infrastructure investment moving forward. The investment can come in multiple forms, the most prevalent being the privatization of the urban water delivery and wastewater management sector. At the beginning of the decade, the global market for water and wastewater treatment was estimated at $160.8 billion, with Australia, Canada, the United States, and the countries of Western Europe accounting for 87 percent of this market.[21] This market will continue to grow, even in the countries already listed. Challenges to access are no longer a concern in these areas, but the water supply needs to be repaired, water treatment technologies expanded, and water storage practices enhanced. For example, the Environmental Protection Agency (EPA) estimates that the current U.S. water infrastructure requires a $334.8 billion capital investment over the next 20 years, broken down as follows: transmission and distribution (60 percent), treatment (22 percent), storage (11 percent), sourcing (6 percent), and other (1 percent).[22] The long-term need is driving a steady increase in spending; The European Union (EU) estimates that $75 billion per year is currently spent on water and wastewater services, and capital is expected to increase by 7 percent annually.[23] As is typical in infrastructure spending, the developed world requires refurbishing and maintenance costs, and the developing world's spending will target the construction of new infrastructure, fueled by the demand for greater water access. The UN's Millennium Development Goal (MDG) sets out a lofty objective for environmental sustainability—cut the number of people without access to safe drinking water and basic sanitation in half by 2015. In order to achieve this, annual water services spending needs to be increased to $180 billion from $75 billion.[24] Even without achieving the UN's MDG, access to water for drinking and sanitation purposes will require spending in the developed world due to rapid urbanization and a lack of infrastructure to support it. As evidence of this trend, private water and sanitation projects in developing countries increased more than fifteenfold (from $2 billion to $35 billion) over the eight-year period between 1992 and 2000.[25]

Private sector participation can lead to new thinking on best-cost solutions in the management of catchment areas and in water supply solutions. Many of the public-private partnerships (PPPs) established in the 1990s in Asia and Eastern Europe found the bias of the public sector utilities in these areas was to increase supply when water shortages occurred. However, by looking initially at how to economically reduce leakage, a faster and more cost-effective solution could be established, which then gave a reasonable amount of time for the operators to plan and implement a new water supply scheme. After all, increasing supply into the same undersized and leaky system would lead to far higher leakage.

Water Rights and Public-Private Partnership Terms

Creating a blueprint for water privatization is difficult. For a start, water rights vary from nation to nation, and thus privatization negations are naturally altered. Some countries treat water and water utilities as public goods under government ownership, while other nations leave water dispersion to private enterprise. Chile, for example, allows for trading of water resources via a system of private ownership, which is independent of land ownership.[26] The Mexican government maintains ownership over water, but leases it in the form of long-term—typically 30-year—concessions.[27] As recently as January 2008, China's legal code did not provide for water ownership, which complicated the water-trading efforts between the North and South. The legal code now provides for water ownership, creating a trading market similar to that of carbon dioxide.[28] England fully privatized its water industry in 1989, resulting in direct competition for water utilities. Some countries have used the private sector to provide specific services as part of the overall water and wastewater systems—for example, Scotland which has wastewater treatment PPPs and Australia which has water treatment PPPs. Due to this discrepancy of state or privately owned water, the terms of privatization vary by transaction, with key differences including the division of responsibility for asset ownership, capital investment, operation, user fee collection, and so on.[29] When contracts are not clearly thought out and enforced by a strong regulatory agency, there can be the potential for different expectations, leading to changes and an erosion of public support.

CASE STUDY: BUENOS AIRES

The privatization of Buenos Aires, Argentina's water supply, presents an interesting example of both the benefits of privatization for public health and development of water supply, as well as the challenges faced in terms of public support, regulatory power, and corporate accountability.

The concession was signed in December of 1992 between the Argentinean government and Aguas Argentinas. Argentinean water rights are held by the government and tied to land ownership, forcing developers to use the water on the land the rights are attached to. Provincial governments can distribute water rights to the private sector through water use concessions.[30]

Prior to the concession, only 70 percent of the Buenos Aires population was connected to the water system, and only 58 percent had access to the sewer system. Approximately 10 percent of the meters providing access were inoperative, further reducing the number of people with actual access to water and sanitation services. From the city's perspective, nearly all the billing was based on factors not related to consumption, and only 80 percent of billing was collected. Equally, the law did not permit the state-owned enterprise, Obras Sanitarias de Mendoz (OSM), from shutting off the water to nonpaying users. The utility was bleeding money, having negative profits in three out of the five preceding years.[31]

The terms of the concession included a 26.9 percentage reduction in prices, and also kept in place the weak tariff authority.[32] Additionally, the Argentinean government was forced to create a division, the User Committee of Ente Tripartito de Obras y Servicios Sanitarios (ETOSS), specifically for the purpose of monitoring the transaction. ETOSS' failure to adequately regulate was one of the deal's greatest weaknesses. ETOSS' independence and legitimacy were soon called into question as its overseers in the national administration approved multiple tariff changes by Aguas Argentinas. Soon after the signing of the tariff, rate increases were enacted. The first came in 1994, and included an increase in rates as well as an increase in the minimum water connection fee by 84 percent and the water infrastructure fee by 38 percent.[33] In Aguas' defense, it was primarily attempting to deflect losses from underperformance, operational losses, and the "extracontractual" cost of speeding up service to poorer neighborhoods.[34] Ironically, these same neighborhoods were the ones primarily impacted by the rate hikes. Over the years, Aguas slowly continued with numerous tariff changes during periods of economic instability, along with much more stringent penalties for payment defaults.[35] Multiple tariff renegotiations were pursued without the consent of ETOSS culminating in the 1997 renegotiation of the contract and depowering of ETOSS. Argentinean president Menem passed Decree 149, taking power from ETOSS and giving it to the Minister of Natural Resources and Sustainable Development.[36] Over time, Aguas began to exert monopolistic power over the fee system, adding steam to the economic downturn that caused the Argentine recession in 1999.[37] Following Argentina's recession, Aguas defaulted on over $700 million.[38] At this point in 2002, water rates had risen 177 percent, albeit with the agreement of the regulator/government.[39] While the Aguas privatization eventually collapsed, there were several positive benefits to the privatization. New connections increased by 11 percent, and coverage increased from 70 percent in 1992 to 83 percent by 1997. Compared to public provision, consumers were better off by almost $1.33 billion (USD).[40] Similarly, according to a 2005 study, privatization resulted in a decrease of 5 percent to 7 percent in infant mortality rates.[41] Studies have argued that privatization resulted in welfare benefits and infrastructure expansion efforts that vastly outweigh the drawbacks.[42] The case of Aguas reveals the importance of a strong central government regulatory agency to control the natural monopoly or pseudo monopoly typical of all infrastructure assets, especially water. The lack of long-term political support that eventually led the government to strip Suez (a leading French-based multinational corporation with operations primarily in water, electricity, and natural gas supply, and waste management) was fueled by Aguas abuses of ETOSS during the regulatory power's youth.

Aguas also gradually isolated itself from the population. The initial privatization was marked by heavy protesting, led by labor union officials. Half of Obres Sanitarias de la Nacion (OSN's) 7,450 workers lost their jobs in the aftermath of privatization, as the workforce was reduced to 4,250, even though indirect employment rose 10 percent when accounting for contract workers from infrastructure expansion.[43] In the final years of the contract, hostility toward both Aguas and the regulatory powers grew due to the lack of competitive bidding and information sharing regarding contractors.[44] Corporate accountability was disappointing, furthering public distrust. Aguas highlights many of the issues facing privatization of water utilities—and infrastructure as a whole—moving forward: the importance of maintaining the public's support while meeting corporate expectations. Aguas was successful at improving access to clean water, yet because of continual tariff hikes, abuse of the ETOSS regulator, and faulty corporate accountability, the corporation was eventually stripped of its partnership contract. As shown through this case study, privatization relies on setting attainable tariffs backed by a strong regulatory authority; by creating the right checks and balances to power, governments can reap the benefits of privatization while ensuring proper care of this politically charged asset.

Desalination

Apart from the privatization of municipal systems, expanding desalination and water treatment programs offer a dynamic infrastructure investment opportunity in the water sector. Many industry professionals categorize these facilities as real assets due to the nature of stable cash flows and municipal contracts, which are common characteristics of infrastructure assets. As the water crisis advances, the opportunity for investing in the global expansion of these technologies will be possible either through public companies or venture capital firms expanding the accuracy of these technologies. Although these systems will by no means eliminate the water shortage crisis, they can significantly reduce water stress and will play a part in averting the potential crisis. Growth in deployment and technological improvements will continue through investment in these technologies.

Desalination is the removal or excess salt and other materials from water, which can then be reused. While water is the largest resource on earth, unfortunately 97.5 percent of it is saltwater or brackish water. In order to bridge the supply-usage gap moving forward, desalination must be employed and capacity enhanced, opening up previously unpotable areas of water for consumption. According to a *Wall Street Journal* article citing the International Desalination Association, 13,080 desalination plants produce in excess of 12 billion gallons of water per day.[45] The Middle East currently dominates desalination efforts, with approximately 75 percent.[46] The largest programs exist in Saudi Arabia and the United Arab Emirates (UAE), the former pumping a little under 600 million gallons a day.[47] Unfortunately, desalination remains less than 1 percent of total global water supply; while a Citibank Water Research Report 2009 estimates this figure will double by 2025, the same source states that this supply growth will have limited effect on dampening the water crisis.[48] The continued growth, however, represents a potential infrastructure opportunity, either through private investment or outsourcing.

The main problem with desalination is it currently lacks the capacity and cost competitiveness for worldwide, large-scale employment. The desalination process needs large amounts of energy to complete the process, and as a consequence is significantly more costly than traditional methods of water supply. This limits much of the current opportunity for desalination plant creation and operations, especially outside the Middle East. For example, the cost of seawater desalination in coastal Southern Californian cities would be no more than 30 percent greater than the current pumping cost of the existing interbasin supply systems. The expansion of desalination is necessary and will continue, but even with substantial growth it will only play a small part in overcoming the impending water deficit.

Wastewater

Wastewater treatment removes the contaminated particles via physical, chemical, or biological means. Water treatment recycles water so that it can be effectively reused, either for drinking, daily function, agriculture, or industry. Like desalination, water treatment solutions have expanded rapidly in an attempt to fill the void created from water stress: a study of 24 cities around the globe found that farmers in 4 out of 5 cities surveyed use wastewater (treated, raw, or diluted) in urban and periurban agriculture.[49] The most profound impact of wastewater treatment is that sewage can be engaged as a resource to help alleviate water stress, as oppose to a waste product. However, the International Water Management Institute (IWMI) argues that outsourcing water quality improvements is an effective mechanism of reducing public health risk.[50]

While water treatment is a viable option, it is still too ineffective at decontaminating water, particularly in the developing world. Many countries in the developing world use untreated wastewater out of necessity to irrigate crops, a treatment that cannot effectively be banned.[51] Reuse of untreated human-related wastewater carries a high risk of passing on disease. Similarly, in the developed world, reuse of treated water has caused public outcry based on socioeconomic grounds. San Diego attempted to establish an 80 ML/day reverse osmosis recycling plant, but was forced to shut down due to a lack of public support for indirect potable consumption. The opposition even falsely claimed that wealthy northern neighborhoods would be distributing treated water to poorer urban communities, inciting racial and socioeconomic inspired fury.[52] Reusing this "greywater" has found more success in dry climates through irrigation of golf courses, public green areas, and limited agriculture. Greywater is wastewater from bathtub, shower drain, sinks, washing machines, and dishwashers. Greywater accounts for 60 percent of the outflow produced in homes. It contains little or no pathogens and 90 percent less nitrogen than black water (toilet water). However, the opportunity for the advancement of water recycling programs remains patent, according to the IWMI. Domestic water can be up to 30 percent to 70 percent of irrigational water use, or 10 percent to 40 percent of total water use in the Middle East, United States, Australia, and parts of Africa. The study argues that since countries already employ wastewater treatment programs (the United States averages 11 percent water recycling in major cities), it will continue to develop as a viable mechanism for water treatment and environmental protection.[53] Recycled wastewater growth estimates differ, with some forecasting that it will be as much as 9 percent of global water supply by 2050.[54] The continued growth of this sector, like desalination, is a measure of cost competitiveness, but global water dynamics indicate that it will be a growing business in the future.

CONCLUSION

The water crisis has some potentially disastrous affects if left unaddressed. The continued global supply shortage and the inadequacy of current water storage mechanisms around the world threaten livelihoods, trade, and industry. Privatization represents one helpful solution to the water problem by increasing access while relieving some of the giant spending demands created by water stress, and in some cases also by lowering the price to the end users. As illustrated through Aguas Argentina, privatization requires a strong regulatory authority able to support the private sectors profit expectations, maintain public support, and adequately control of this natural monopoly. Aside from privatization, investment in the growing technologies used for water treatment, conservation, and recycling offers another means of access to this attractive market. Water supply will become an increasing problem over the next century. Spending requirements to rehabilitate existing infrastructure are too hefty for the public sector to absorb moving forward, and private investment in water infrastructure will help deflect some of these costs. In order to maximize the potential success of these privatization opportunities, both governments and corporations need to set realistic expectations and work together during both economic affluence and decline. The problem requires a two-sector solution.

ENDNOTES

1. World Water Forum: "Diverse Background and Perspectives United for Water Management." Republic of the Philippines Department of Environment and Natural Resources Environmental Management Bureau. Available at www.emb.gov.ph/. Accessed 11/20/2009.
2. UNEP (2002), "Vital Water Graphics—An Overview of the State of the World's Fresh and Marine Waters." UNEP, Nairobi, Kenya. ISBN: 9280722360.
3. World Water Assessment Program 2003. "Water for People, The United Nations World Water Development Report: Water For Life." UNESCO, and London: Earthscan. Available at www.unesco.org/water/wwdr/ex_summary. Accessed 11/20/2009.
4. World Water Forum: "Diverse Background and Perspectives United for Water Management."
5. The Millennium Development Goals Report 2008, published by the United Nations Department of Economic and Social Affairs, August 2008. Available at www.un.org/millenniumgoals. Accessed 11/20/2009.
6. The United Nations World Water Development Report 3: "Water in a Changing World." Paris: UNESCO, and London: Earthscan.
7. Zygmunt, Joanne. "Hidden Waters." Briefing from WaterWise, produced February 2007.
8. Allan, J.A. *Virtual Water: An Essential Element in Stabilizing the Political Economies of the Middle East,* Yale School of Forestry Bulletin 103: *Transformations of Middle Eastern Natural Environments: Legacies and Lessons,* New Haven, CT: Yale University Press 1998. Page 141–150.
9. The United Nations World Water Development Report 3: "Water in a Changing World."

10. Alcazar, Lorena, Abdala, Manuel, and Shirley, Mary. "The Buenos Aires Water Concession." The World Bank Development Research Group: Regulation and Competition Policy, April 2000.
11. McCully, Patrick. *Silenced Rivers: The Ecology and Politics of Large Dams.* Zed Books: 2001, page 349.
12. Atkins, William Arthur. "Hydroelectric Power." Water Encyclopedia article Available at www.waterencyclopedia.com/Ge-Hy/Hydroelectric-Power.html. Accessed 11/19/2009.
13. World Water Forum: "Diverse Background and Perspectives United for Water Management."
14. "How a Hydroelectric Plant can Affect a River." Foundation for Water and Energy Education. Available at www.fwee.org/hpar.html. Accessed 11/23/2009.
15. McCully, Patrick. *Silenced Rivers: The Ecology and Politics of Large Dams.*
16. OECD Environmental Outlook to 2030, March 5, 2008. ISBN: 9789264040489. Available at www.oecd.org/document/20/0,3343,en_2649_34305_39676628_1_1_1_37465,00.html. Accessed 11/23/2009.
17. Kerschner, Edward M. and Geraghty, Michael. "Water Worries #2: The Rising Risk of 'Water Bankruptcy.'" Citigroup Global Markets, May 20 2009.
18. OECD Environmental Outlook to 2030, page 349.
19. Jenkins, Marion W., Tanaka, Stacy K., Zhu, Tingju, Lund, Jay R., Howitt, Richard E., Pulido, Manuel A., Tauber, Mélanie, Ritzema Randall S., and Ferreira, Inês C. "Climate Warming and Water Management Adaptation for California." *Springer Netherlands* volume 76 Numbers 3-4, June 2006.
20. "A Shortage of Capital Flows: Going Thirsty so Beijing Can Drink," *The Economist*, October 9th 2008. Available at www.economist.com/world/asia/displaystory.cfm?story_id=12376698. Accessed 11/19/2009.
21. Baumert, Jennifer and Bloodgood, Laura. "Private Sector Participation in the Water and Wastewater Service Industry." Office of Industries – US International Trade Commission Working Paper, April 2004. Available at Department of State Telegram www.usitc.gov/publications/332/working papers/wp id 08.pdf. Accessed 11/19/2009.
22. EPA's 2007 Drinking Water Infrastructure Needs Survey and Assessment. Published by EPA Office of Water, February 2009. Available at www.epa.gov/safewater. Accessed 11/23/2009.
23. OECD Environmental Outlook to 2030, page 349.
24. Global Water Partnership, "Report of the World Panel on Financing Water Infrastructure," 2003.
25. The Millennium Development Goals Report 2008.
26. The International Bank for Reconstruction and Development and The World Bank. "Labor Issues in Infrastructure Reform: A Tool Kit." Modules 2–7. 2004. Available at http://rru.worldbank.org/documents/toolkits/labor/toolkit/download_modules.html. Accessed 11/23/2009.
27. Baumert, Jennifer and Bloodgood, Laura. "Private Sector Participation in the Water and Wastewater Service Industry."

28. Jigang, Zhou, Guangcan, Peter, and Zhen, Ceng. "Trading water in thirsty China." *China Dialogue*, June 26, 2008. Available at www.chinadialogue.net/article/show/single/en/2144. Accessed 11/23/2009.
29. OECD Environmental Outlook to 2030. Ibid.
30. Baumert, Jennifer and Bloodgood, Laura. "Private Sector Participation in the Water and Wastewater Service Industry."
31. Oletta, Andres. "The World Bank's Influence on Water Privatisation in Argentina: The Experience of the City of Buenos Aires." International Environmental Law Research Centre Working Paper, 2007.
32. Ibid.
33. Ibid.
34. CBC news. Argentina: *A Grand Experiment in Water Privatization that Failed*. Originally broadcast on March 31, 2004. Available at www.cbc.ca/fifth/deadinthewater/argentina.html. Accessed 11/20/2009.
35. Santoro, Daniel. "The 'Aguas' Tango." Global Policy Forum, February 6, 2003.
36. CBC news. Argentina: *A Grand Experiment in Water Privatization that Failed*. Originally broadcast on March 31, 2004. Available at www.cbc.ca/fifth/deadinthewater/argentina.html. Accessed 11/20/2009.
37. Oletta, Andres. "The World Bank's Influence on Water Privatisation in Argentina: The Experience of the City of Buenos Aires."
38. Baumert, Jennifer and Bloodgood, Laura. "Private Sector Participation in the Water and Wastewater Services Industry."
39. CBC news. *Argentina: A Grand Experiment in Water Privatization that Failed*.
40. Alcazar, Lorena, Abdala, Manuel, and Shirley, Mary. "The Buenos Aires Water Concession."
41. Galiani S, Gertler P, Schargrodsky E, Sturzenegger F. "The Costs and Benefits of Privatization: Geopolitical Water Issues Likely to Arise in the World during the Next Two Decades." World Economic Forum January 2009.
42. McKenzie D, Mookherjee D. "The Distributive Impact of Privatization in Latin America: Evidence from Four Countries." *Economia*. 2003; 3(2):161–233.
43. The International Bank for Reconstruction and Development and The World Bank. "Labor Issues in Infrastructure Reform: A Tool Kit." Modules 2–7.
44. Wu, Xun and Malaluan, Nepomuceno A. A Tale of Two Concessionaires: A Natural Experiment of Water Privatisation in Metro Manila. Urban Stud 2008; 45; 207. Available at http://usj.sagepub.com/cgi/content/abstract/45/1/207. Accessed 11/23/2009.
45. International Desalination Association, Kranhold, Katherine. "Water, Water, Everywhere." *Wall Street Journal*, January 17, 2008. Available (subscription required) at http://online.wsj.com/article/SB120053698876396483.html?mod=googlenews_wsj.
46. Fischetti, Mark. "Fresh from the Sea." *Scientific American*, September 2007. Available at www.scientificamerican.com/article.cfm?id=fresh-from-the-sea. Accessed 11/20/2009.
47. Hunter, Norrie. "Geographic Focus—Middle East: Providing Water and Water Infrastructure to the Desert." Working with Water Feature. August 13, 2009. Available at www.workingwithwater.net/view/3225/geographic-focus-middle-east-providing-water-and-water-infrastructure-to-the-desert-/Palm Water Study. Accessed 11/23/2009.

48. Kerschner, Edward M. and Geraghty, Michael. "Water Worries #2: The Rising Risk of 'Water Bankruptcy.'"
49. Molle, F., and Berkoff, J. "Cities versus Agriculture: Revisiting Intersectoral Water Transfers, Potential Gains and Conflicts."Comprehensive Assessment Research Report 10, Colombo, Sri Lanka: International Water Management Institute.
50. Raschid-Sally, L., Jayakody, P. 2008. "Drivers and Characteristics of Wastewater Agriculture in Developing Countries: Results from a Global Assessment." Colombo, Sri Lanka: International Water Management Institute, page 35. (IWMI Research Report 127).
51. Ibid.
52. Sheikh, B. (2003). Indirect Potable Reuse through Groundwater Recharge and Surface Water Augmentation: The Gold Standard of Water Recycling for California, CD-ROM, Water Recycling Australia, 2nd National Conference 1–3 September, 2003 Brisbane. Australian Water Association, Sydney.
53. Raschid-Sally, L., Jayakody, P. 2008. "Drivers and Characteristics of Waste water Agriculture in Developing Countries: Results from a Global Assessment."
54. Kerschner, Edward M. and Geraghty, Michael. "Water Worries #2: The Rising Risk of 'Water Bankruptcy.'"

CHAPTER 6

Master Limited Partnerships

David N. Fleischer
Principal, Chickasaw Capital Management, LLC

Matthew G. Mead
Principal, Chickasaw Capital Management, LLC

Robert M.T. Walker
Research Analyst, Chickasaw Capital Management, LLC

James L. Johnstone
Vice President, Chickasaw Capital Management, LLC

INTRODUCTION

Master Limited Partnerships (MLPs) are significant owners of the United States' energy infrastructure, controlling approximately $250 billion of assets involved in the transportation, processing, and storage of the nation's energy needs. These assets include major pipeline systems that deliver energy products such as natural gas, crude oil, and refined petroleum products to end markets; thus, nearly all other critical infrastructure is directly dependent upon the products that MLPs deliver.

MLPs offer investors important investment attributes that make them a compelling infrastructure investment class. First, MLPs have historically exhibited strong performance when compared to the broader equity markets, with lower risk, and low correlation to other asset classes (see Exhibit 6.1). Second, MLPs pay quarterly cash distributions to investors, which provide attractive current yields. The distributions that investors receive from most MLPs are stable and predictable because their business models are

EXHIBIT 6.1 Total Returns for U.S. Asset Indices, January 2000–December 2008

Index[1]	Annualized Return (%)	Annualized Standard Deviation (%)	Beta[2]	Correlation[3] (%)	Sharpe Ratio[4]	Positive Months (%)	Largest Monthly Drawdown (%)	Largest Yearly Drawdown (%)	Largest Cumulative Drawdown[5] (%)
Citigroup MLP	14.04%	15.98%	0.31	100.00%	0.69	67.59%	−16.53%	−36.77%	−41.96%
S&P 500	−3.60	15.22	1.00	32.84	−0.43	56.48	−16.79	−37.00	−44.73
DJIA	−0.82	14.79	0.97	27.63	−0.26	53.70	−13.88	−31.93	−34.83
NASDAQ	−9.48	27.24	0.46	28.82	−0.46	49.07	−22.89	−39.98	−74.85
RUSSELL 2000	1.23	20.56	0.57	37.11	−0.08	55.56	−20.80	−33.79	−42.97
MSCI World	−2.94	15.55	0.94	32.84	0.38	55.56	−18.94	−40.40	−47.48
S&P GSCI	4.15	25.50	0.09	23.71	0.05	55.56	−28.20	−46.49	−62.16
NAREIT	8.85	20.93	0.37	29.65	0.28	67.59	−31.67	−37.73	−58.40

Notes:
[1] Statistics based on total return indices
[2] Relative to the S&P 500 calculated over the whole period (monthly data) based on excess returns over 30 days T-Bills
[3] Relative to the Citigroup MLP Index
[4] Measured using returns in excess over 30 days T-Bills
[5] Using month-end data only
Source: Bloomberg data, December 31, 2008.

dominated by fee-based, tariff oriented revenues from businesses that are near monopolistic and supported by inelastic U.S. energy demand. Lastly, MLPs offer the liquidity and flexibility of being publicly traded. The strong investment attributes of MLPs make a compelling case for investors to more frequently favor MLPs when considering infrastructure allocations.

An MLP is a publicly traded entity that trades on the major U.S. stock exchanges and conforms to the same accounting, reporting principles and SEC regulations as any publicly traded corporation. The Revenue Act of 1987 limited publicly traded MLPs to the income and capital gains from natural resource activities such as: exploration, development, mining or production, processing, refining, transportation (including pipelines transporting gas, oil, or products thereof); the marketing of any mineral or natural resource (including fertilizer, geothermal energy, and timber); rental income and capital gains from real estate; and income from commodity investments as detailed in Section 7704 of the Internal Revenue Code. An MLP may be organized as either a limited partnership or as a limited liability company, and enjoys the tax treatment of a partnership in which all tax items, including depreciation, pass fully to their unit holders through an annual Schedule K-1 filing provided by the MLP to the unit holder. Because of the MLP's partnership tax status, MLP investors avoid the double taxation experienced by shareholders of regular corporations. A partnership that does not generate 90 percent or more of its gross income from qualifying sources is treated as a corporation for tax purposes.

MLPs that are structured as limited partnerships (LPs) have general partners (GPs). Through this structure, GPs benefit in two ways. First, GPs control the ultimate direction of the partnership through their control of the governance rights. Second, GPs receive incentive distribution rights (IDRs) when an MLP hits certain distribution cash flow targets. IDRs are meant to encourage the growth of MLPs for the benefit of both GP and LP unit holders, and the IDR structure has served many MLPs well as they have experienced significant growth over the past decade. But IDRs also have the potential to become onerous as the GP takes an increasingly larger portion of the cash flows available for distribution. It should be noted that certain GPs are publicly traded allowing retail and institutional investors to participate in this economic relationship. The strong returns that MLP investors have enjoyed are based on a two primary factors; yield and growth. MLPs have consistently traded in the public market with distribution yields of 6 percent to 7 percent. Through modest growth in energy demand along with an attractive rate structure, MLPs have delivered growth of 4 percent to 8 percent annually over the past 20 years. The combination of yield plus growth has allowed MLP investors to enjoy low double digit returns.

MLPs own and operate some of the most important energy infrastructure in the United States. Most MLP assets are focused on fee-based midstream energy infrastructure such as pipeline, terminal, and storage assets. Inelastic demand for energy products is expected to continue to increase the need for new pipelines, storage facilities, and terminal assets throughout the United States. According to the Energy Information Administration (EIA), petroleum products and natural gas energy demand grew at a 1.50 percent compounded rate from 1980 to 2007, and is expected to continue to increase over the long term.[1] This GDP-related growth, coupled with inelastic demand, provides a robust foundation enjoyed by midstream energy MLPs.

MLPs are well positioned to grow through their significant participation in the build-out and consolidation of U.S. energy infrastructure. It is estimated that the United States needs hundreds of billions of dollars in new natural gas, crude oil, and refined products infrastructure over the next decade. MLPs are also a likely buyer of many of the midstream energy infrastructure assets currently owned in both private and public corporate entities. Additionally, the MLP structure is well positioned for hundreds of billions of dollars more in new forms of energy infrastructure brought by technological advancements. These assets include liquefied natural gas terminals, gas-to-liquids technologies, biofuel assets, renewable energy assets, and coal gasification projects. For instance, the cost of implementing clean coal technology alone could cost $1 trillion.[2]

There are currently 78 publicly traded Energy MLPs:

- 44 Pipelines/Midstream Operations: Long-Haul Natural Gas, Refined Products, Processing and Gathering
- 26 Commodity-Sensitive: Propane and Heating Oil, Exploration and Production, Coal
- 8 Marine Transportation

Midstream Energy MLPs bear the closest resemblance to a toll road business model. Most do not take ownership of the commodities transported and cash flows for many midstream MLPs are minimally influenced by the fluctuations in commodity prices. Many midstream MLPs typically receive a capacity reservation fee paid by a local utility to guarantee product delivery, however the fee can also be received from shippers who want to ensure their products reach end markets which minimizes the issue of volume dependency ("take or pay" contracts). This type of contract provides stable cash flow and limits their credit risk as commodity prices fluctuate.

Fees are both regulated or market determined depending on areas of operation. The Federal Energy Regulatory Commission (FERC) has allowed certain tariff-based MLPs to incorporate a Producer Price Index (PPI) "plus" fee rate adjustment structure when determining annual tariff rates. Many other contracts, particularly storage, are tied to Consumer Price Index (CPI). Market rates among nontariff-based MLPs are often influenced by the PPI and CPI adjustments incorporated by tariff based MLPs. On occasion, FERC will arbitrate market rates when there is a conflict between customer and service provider. Historically, FERC has been light-handed in their regulation and has allowed markets to determine rates among nontariff-based MLPs.

MLPs provide a valuable inflation hedge within an infrastructure portfolio in three distinct ways. First, by having market rates for both tariff and nontariff assets tied to government-reported inflation measures such as PPI and CPI, cash flows are not diluted in an inflationary world. Second, infrastructure assets traditionally provide an element of inflation-hedging through the replacement cost of long-lived hard assets and/or GDP growth associated with increased asset use. Lastly, MLPs involved in businesses such as propane, heating oil, exploration and production, coal, and certain gathering and processing activities, have more seasonal and commodity sensitivity associated with their cash flows. MLPs involved in these sectors allow the investor to increase the inflation-hedging capabilities within one's portfolio by increasing the portfolio allocation to MLPs involved with these more commodity-sensitive businesses.

In addition to certain MLPs that possess commodity price exposure, all energy-oriented MLPs are subject to energy risks. Changes in end-user demand for energy products or innovative energy alternatives could substitute the need for transportation, processing, and storage through the existing infrastructure owned by MLPs. Lower commodity prices affect certain MLPs in two ways. First, lower commodity prices may negatively affect drilling programs and the production profile in producing fields which could impact future MLP growth projects. Second, for those gathering and processing MLPs with equity volumes in their contracts, lower commodity prices on natural gas and natural gas liquids could lead to lower margins. It is important that MLPs with equity volume sensitivity maintain effective and detailed hedging programs to protect cash flow and distributions.

Consideration should be given to the structural risks, such as the regulatory, legislative, and capital structure risks associated with MLPs. FERC is charged with regulating interstate tariff rates and regulating many MLPs' business. Changes in current regulatory policies could have an adverse impact on these businesses. Should Congress change the pass-through nature of limited partnerships or make other unfavorable changes to regulations in the tax code, MLPs could be adversely affected. MLPs typically pay out most of their annual cash flow in the form of quarterly cash distributions.

Therefore, MLPs have a perpetual reliance on external equity and debt financing to fund growth, which requires strong creditworthiness. In addition, it is important to consider the term structure of debt and any covenant restriction an MLP may face.

MLPs have demonstrated a variety of compelling strengths and attributes over a long time period balanced with modest risk. As an investor considers how to implement an infrastructure allocation, it is clear that MLPs should be carefully considered as a component of one's overall infrastructure portfolio. MLPs possess many strengths including: (1) strong historical returns with low risk and low correlation to other assets; (2) cash distributions paid quarterly at an attractive yield; (3) strong inflation hedging through (a) market rates that are inflation indexed, (b) replacement cost of long-lived, high-value physical assets most of which operate with natural monopolies, and (c) exposure through certain MLPs with direct commodity price exposure; (4) portfolio flexibility through the liquidity and transparency of being publicly traded; (5) history of private ownership of energy infrastructure assets limits political or public risk often found in other infrastructure projects, such as toll road or airport ownership conversions from public to private ownership.

MLPs represent an attractive investment opportunity that should be considered as a core holding within any investor's infrastructure allocation.

THE PAST

Early Years

The modern MLP era began with the passage of the Tax Reform Act of 1986. Buckeye Partners, LP (NYSE: BPL), a refined products pipeline, became the first modern MLP when it was organized as a publicly traded MLP in December 1986. Buckeye established the basic formula for the development of publicly traded MLPs. The public was introduced to a partnership that had a visible, predictable refined-products-pipeline business whose yield-oriented investors could have confidence in a stable, growing quarterly cash distribution. Investors could count on a monopoly-like pipeline to deliver steady, visible cash flow that funded a consistent and growing distribution. Investors found stability and predictability in a low-risk, fee-based business model that delivered refined petroleum products to cities in the northeastern United States.

The development of the publicly traded MLP marketplace followed a simple formula of bringing to market partnerships with fee-based midstream energy assets, such as pipelines, that generated stable, predictable cash flow. Early MLPs had hard assets with high barriers to entry that enabled highly predictable cash flow. Established and, in many cases, near-monopoly business franchises also supported consistent growth. Throughput increases were leveraged into even higher income and cash flow gains since most costs remained fixed. Product pipelines had the advantage of grandfathered rates that were reasonable and included inflationary rate increases. Energy demand continued to grow with U.S. population and gross domestic product (GDP) growth; however, the inelasticity of energy demand shielded MLP earnings from economic volatility. Investors expected and received a low double-digit return that was enabled by both a healthy cash yield and modest organic growth.

Kinder Morgan Energy Partners, LP

A new era in MLPs began with the formation of Kinder Morgan Energy Partners, LP (NYSE: KMP) in February of 1997, when a group of investors, led by Chairman and CEO Richard D. Kinder and former Vice Chairman William V. Morgan, acquired the general partner of a small, publicly traded pipeline limited partnership, Enron Liquids Pipeline, LP.

Kinder built upon the basic ingredients of MLPs and demonstrated through accretive acquisitions and organic growth projects that an MLP did not have to settle for delivering a low double-digit total return to investors. Kinder produced an enviable track record: a compound growth rate of 26 percent[3] from its inception through May of 2009. KMP has increased its quarterly cash distribution 35 times since 1997 and is the largest MLP, with an enterprise value of approximately $20 billion and over 8000 employees (see Exhibit 6.2).

Recent Past

The basic MLP formula has expanded over the past few years to include a wider variety of business models engaged in shipping, coal, and oil and gas exploration and production. These businesses have different investment considerations when compared to the traditional base of midstream energy infrastructure assets that were the exclusive asset base of the early years and still dominate the MLP universe today. These newer businesses may have more commodity price sensitivity or a shorter expected life of the assets. Because of the introduction of these additional investment considerations, investors should closely monitor and be mindful that cash flow streams can be more volatile and less predictable than those associated with midstream energy assets.

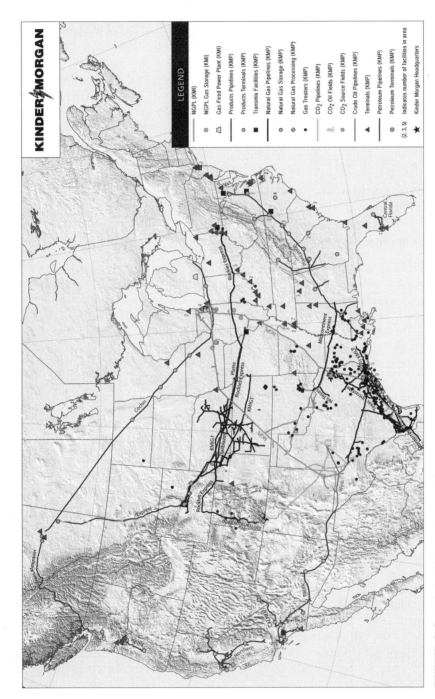

EXHIBIT 6.2 Kinder Morgan System Map

Source: Used with permission of Kinder Morgan.

THE PRESENT

Fundamentals

Whereas the previous three to five years witnessed investors placing a premium on partnerships that demonstrated above average growth and worrying less about potential volatility of certain MLPs' cash flows, the present state of MLPs reflects a shifting bifurcation of investor attitudes. Today, investors place a meaningful premium on investment grade-rated partnerships, typically larger MLPs involved in long-haul transportation, storage, and terminaling that can access debt and equity funding markets due more stable operating models.

Current underlying trends for MLPs are mixed depending on the nature of their business. The partnerships that engage in long-haul transportation and storage have experienced some demand weakness associated with the consumer recession, but have offset this weakness due to reservation fees (take or pay contracts), the inflation escalators tied to PPI/CPI which took effect mid-year 2009 at approximately 7.5 percent, or the rolling of storage contracts into a strong, contango (future price is greater than current) oil market.

The noninvestment-grade gatherers and processors have experienced greater operational stress as producers pull back from drilling commitments in all but the most prolific shale basins. This has reduced both fee-based and equity-based volumes, but because many of these partnerships engaged in significant hedging programs (typically put in place during the higher commodity price periods of 2008), they have offset a good deal of the superficial volumetric drops. Additionally, as commodity prices linked to the price of oil recovered over the first half of 2009 from late 2008s epic collapse (see Exhibit 6.3), gatherers and processors have received higher prices for unhedged volumes or put new, higher hedges in place to protect their cash flows, distributions, and balance sheets.

Outside of the midstream sector, the underlying results have been mixed. Propane MLPs benefitted greatly during the 2009 winter heating season as they captured a greater margin between what they paid for product versus what price they sold it. Exploration and Production (E&P) MLPs, for the most part, have protected their 2009 cash flows with 2008 priced hedges, but borrowing base redeterminations on the value of their underlying properties due to lower current oil and gas prices reduced availability on certain credit lines. This, in turn, has forced some distribution cuts or suspensions as E&P MLPs focus on paying down debt. Coal MLPs have experienced similar volatility to E&P MLPs due to lower market prices for coal. Shipping MLPs confronted lower re-contracting rates and shorter durations.

EXHIBIT 6.3 Historical Processing Margin and Crude-to-Gas Ratio: Jan 1, 2004–June 30, 2009
Source: Bloomberg data, June 2009.

Future organic growth in the form of new projects across the midstream sector has continued but at a more measured pace. Large investment-grade MLPs continue to fund long-haul natural gas transportation pipelines, build natural gas and oil storage with long-term contracts (over 10 years) for refiners and producers, and replace midstream projects that producer customers can no longer fund internally due to capital constraints. These projects notwithstanding, overall spending is, generally speaking, down 20 percent to 25 percent.

As lower commodity prices have forced lower flow rates from existing wells and shut-ins of unprofitable wells, the available slate of projects for the gatherer and processors has diminished considerably. Additionally, cash flow and balance sheet weakness at certain partnerships has reduced organic construction to nil at some partnerships. Those negatives aside, gatherers and processors with operations in and around the shale plays still have opportunities to build takeaway capacity as producer customers focus the bulk of their drilling dollars in these areas. There is also a role for gatherers and processors, similar to their larger midstream brethren, to construct new capacity for more stable producers who were previously funding their gathering and processing capabilities internally.

Organic spending at nonmidstream MLPs has never been a strong historical component as the majority of the partnerships have been growth-by-acquisition models. High cost of capital issues has temporarily suspended this type of model, and whatever organic spending was occurring (mostly at E&P MLPs through the drill bit) has been reduced to only the lowest cost project opportunities.

Similar to their operational differences, capital structure and balance sheet construction has varied in 2009 depending on one's investment-grade status. Even though most partnerships (rated and nonrated) in the midstream have maintained, on average, 50 percent debt-to-capital ratios and 3.0 to 4.0 times leverage, the nature of certain partnerships' cash flows showed how quickly leverage can ruin a balance sheet as debt stays fixed but cash flows greatly diminish. Gatherer and processors who receive a higher percentage of their cash flows tied to commodity prices and drilling activity have therefore seen the greatest reduction in cash flow visibility, and the highest amount of scrutiny around their leverage.

Partnerships with a greater reliance on bank credit lines rather than the capital markets for debt funding have experienced the greatest amount of stress, too. This has been quite symptomatic in the gatherer and processors. Concerns have been both speculated and real in this group that partnerships would be confronted with either technical default on bank credit lines or would have future distributions significantly reduced or temporarily suspended as they worked with bank creditors to obtain credit waivers on covenant issues related to leverage and/or interest coverage. Debt stress has compounded capital structure issues because it also cuts off the ability of these nonrated partnerships to fund the equity side of their balance sheets with new units to keep debt and equity in balance as new equity investors are unwilling to accept what could be significant dilution.

For investment-grade midstream companies, concerns have been present that they would be unable to access debt markets to either roll maturities or fund new projects. However, these MLPs have proven that even during the worst of market environments, such as the fourth quarter of 2008, that access to debt markets was indeed available. While credit spreads were significantly elevated versus historical observations, over $2 billion of debt was priced in December 2008. Credit spreads have since narrowed significantly and are closer to historical norms. In fact, some companies have used this period of relative strength to prefund the debt side of future projects, and potentially, acquisitions. The ability to access public debt markets, linearly, has given investment-grade midstream MLPs access to additional equity financing to keep their balance sheets at balanced funding percentages. Among all MLPs, there has been $7.45 billion of debt raised between December 2008 and June 30, 2009 (see Exhibit 6.4).

There has been a significant difference between investment-grade and noninvestment-grade rated debt yields as demonstrated by spreads

EXHIBIT 6.4 Debt Raised by MLPs: December 2008–June 30, 2009

Issuance Date	Issuer	Offering Amount ($mm)	Coupon	YTM	Dur. (Yrs.)	Type	S&P Rating
12/3/2008	Enterprise Product Ptrs	500.0	9.750%	9.750%	6	Sr. Notes	BBB–
12/17/2008	Kinder Morgan Energy Ptrs	500.0	9.000%	9.000%	10	Sr. Notes	BBB
12/17/2008	Enbridge Energy Ptrs	500.0	9.875%	9.875%	10	Sr. Notes	BBB
12/18/2008	Energy Transfer Ptrs	600.0	9.700%	9.700%	10	Sr. Notes	BBB–
1/8/2009	Inergy LP	225.0	8.750%	8.750%	6	Sr. Notes	BB–
2/6/2009	Sunoco Logistics Ptrs	175.0	8.750%	8.750%	5	Sr. Notes	BBB
2/27/2009	ONEOK Ptrs	500.0	8.625%	8.625%	10	Sr. Notes	BBB
3/27/2009	Natural Resource Ptrs	50.0	8.920%	8.920%	15	Sr. Notes	NR
3/27/2009	Natural Resource Ptrs	150.0	8.380%	8.380%	10	Sr. Notes	NR
4/2/2009	Energy Transfer Ptrs	350.0	8.500%	8.500%	5	Sr. Notes	BBB–
4/2/2009	Energy Transfer Ptrs	650.0	9.000%	9.000%	10	Sr. Notes	BBB–
4/15/2009	Plains All American Pipeline	350.0	8.750%	8.750%	10	Sr. Notes	BBB–
5/8/2009	Kinder Morgan Energy Ptrs	300.0	5.625%	5.625%	5	Sr. Notes	BBB
5/8/2009	Kinder Morgan Energy Ptrs	700.0	6.850%	6.850%	10	Sr. Notes	BBB
5/13/2009	Linn Energy, LLC	250.0	11.750%	12.750%	8	Sr. Notes	B+
5/15/2009	Regency Energy Prs	250.0	9.375%	10.500%	7	Sr. Notes	BB–
5/20/2009	MarkWest Energy Ptrs	150.0	6.875%	12.500%	5	Sr. Notes	B+
6/1/2009	Enterprise Product Ptrs	500.0	4.600%	4.600%	3	Sr. Notes	BBB–
6/19/2009	Magellan Midstream Ptrs	500.0	6.550%	6.550%	10	Sr. Notes	BBB
6/29/2009	Targa Resource Ptrs	250.0	11.250%	12.250%	8	Sr. Notes	B
December 2008–June 30, 2009 Total		**7,450.0**					
2009 YTD		**5,350.0**					

Source: Individual company filings and Bloomberg data, June 2009.

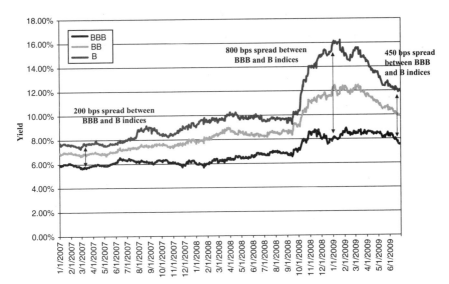

EXHIBIT 6.5 Corporate Yield Differentials, January 2007–June 2009
Source: Bloomberg data, June 2009.

between the various corporate bond indices (see Exhibit 6.5), and this can be used to graphically illustrate similar differences between investment-grade and noninvestment-grade rated partnerships. MLP equity valuations as expressed through lower equity yields are influenced by lower debt yields. Since a partnership's cost of capital is determined by both the cost of debt and cost of equity, if both parts of the balance sheet are priced more expensively than other MLPs in the market, that MLP will be a competitive disadvantage. The partnership's ability to fund organic capital spending projects can be materially affected due to significant cost of capital differences between investment grade and noninvestment grade partnerships.

Although investment grade partnerships have seen a rise in their cost of capital, most have obtained higher rates of return to keep the spread they expect to earn above their projects' cost consistent with historical results. Noninvestment grade partnerships have chosen not to access the capital markets until recently when funding has attained levels that fall back within their parameters for earning a minimum return. For many projects planned by noninvestment grade companies, the higher cost of capital has led to outright cancellation of previously budgeted opportunities.

For midstream companies with still-attractive rates of return on organic projects even with higher debt and equity funding rates, entering into joint ventures (JVs) with well-funded partnerships has become another viable option. In one instance, MarkWest Energy Partners (NYSE: MWE) contributed their existing Appalachian assets to a new joint venture with NGP Midstream & Resources (who contributed cash), in order to develop gathering and processing infrastructure in the Marcellus Shale. In another, Regency Gas Partners (NASDAQ: RGNC), joint ventured with GE Capital and Alinda Partners by contributing its RIGS System in northwest Louisiana to be the backbone of a new interstate pipeline project to take gas out of the Haynesville Shale.

Distributions

Since individual investors own approximately 75 percent of all MLPs units, distributions are the most important consideration for the majority of MLP investors. Individual investors are primarily motivated by the cash distributions, so their first priority is determining their annual distribution yield.

As compared to the environment of higher historical annual distribution growth rates (10 percent to 12 percent) of the previous five years, the current environment will witness more moderate growth in distributions but should still grow at 3.5 percent to 4.5 percent. The expected distribution growth rate offered by today's environment is consistent with the experience that investors had throughout much of the 1990s when annual distribution growth rates were 4 percent to 6 percent. It is important to look at the individual MLPs because the growth rates vary from 10 percent to 12 percent at the high end, versus 0 percent or a suspended distribution (100 percent cut) at the more stressed partnerships which were discussed earlier. Distribution coverage ratios (Distributable Cash Flow/Distribution) have remained well above 1.0 times (100 percent coverage), and in the investment grade category, have increased from 1.0 times to 1.1 times historically to 1.1 times to 1.2 times as partnerships retain more cash for self-funding purposes and as a result of overall economic uncertainty. In the gatherer and processor space, distributions and a partnership's ability to cover the distribution 100 percent have been questioned due to recent economic conditions. The general partners of the limited partnerships have provided various levels of support to maintain distributions at the current level. The support has most notably come in the form of the suspension of general partners' Incentive Distribution Rights (IDRs).

Valuations

Overview   When valuing MLPs, it is important to note the majority of noninsider owners are individual investors who hold MLPs for their yield and are less focused on other forms of valuation. This breeds an environment where investors become more focused on the relative value of MLPs (by comparing yields) rather than the intrinsic value of MLPs that focuses more on the longevity of cash flows. Consequently, long-term opportunities can be created out of short-term haste for both institutional and retail investors with a longer investment horizon.

Following the collapse of Lehman Brothers in September 2008 and the ensuing market volatility, MLPs became very cheap across all valuation metrics. While their yields alone signaled distress across both investment-grade and noninvestment-grade partnerships, underlying cash flows showed that tremendous investment opportunities were at hand. Currently, yields remain elevated versus history, cash flows remain mostly strong, and the environment presents investors with private-equity type total returns (yield + growth) in the low to mid teens on a percentage basis.

Yield   As mentioned, the most watched valuation measure of MLPs is the current yield. When compared to history, MLP yields measured against the 10-year Treasury yield remain high and still have room for reversion just to the historical mean.

Similar to operating statistics, the stronger results and higher degree of stability from the investment grade partnerships has been reflected in the disparity in yields among the midstream sector. Yields are simply:

$$Current\ Yield = \left(\frac{Current\ Dividend\ Per\ Share \times 4}{Current\ Price} \right)$$

Ultimately, investors are willing to receive lower yields for a higher certainty that the current distribution will continue to be paid. This is a change of course from the previous five years when investors place a higher premium (lower yield) on companies that promised distribution growth of 10 percent to 20 percent for a period of time. Now that those higher growth rates are less certain in this period of economic and commodity price weakness, investors have placed lower yields on partnerships with greater distribution certainty.

Distributable Cash Flow (DCF)   The other most common component of valuation that should matter more to investors but is frequently overlooked in favor of yield is the distributable cash flow (DCF). DCF is the amount of cash that a partnership generates, measured quarterly and annually, from which they can pay the distribution. The distribution is then measured in relation to the distribution or the *coverage ratio*, or DCF/distribution = coverage ratio. In this example (Exhibits 6.6–6.8), distributable cash can

EXHIBIT 6.6   Sample Income Statement

Income Statement	(*in $ mm*)
Revenue	50,000
Expenses	30,000
Gross margin	20,000
Selling, general and administrative	5,000
Depreciation and amoritization	10,000
Operating income	5,000
Interest expense	3,000
Income before taxes	2,000
Taxes	0
Net income	2,000
Supplemental	
Maintenance capital expenditures	2,000
Distributions	9,000

be measured going down the income statement as well as building back up using net income.

There is an important distinction to note when discussing DCF and free cash flow. DCF is cash that is available for distribution but is not a perfect measure of free cash flow. This is because MLPs are dependent upon financing markets to cover the majority of the growth capital expenditure portion of their budgets, whereas free cash flow, as typically measured, is cash from operations less *all* capital expenditures including any growth

EXHIBIT 6.7   Distributable Cash Flow—Top Down

Operating income	$ 5,000
Depreciation and amortization	+10,000
EBITDA	15,000
Interest expense	−3,000
Maintenance capital expenditures	−2,000
Distributable cash flow	10,000
Distributions	9,000
Coverage	1.11x

Note: Dollar amounts in millions

EXHIBIT 6.8 Distributable Cash Flow—Bottom Up

Net income	$ 2,000
Depreciation and amortization	+10,000
Maintenance capital expenditures	−2,000
Distributable cash flow	10,000
Distributions	9,000
Coverage	1.11x

Note: Dollar amounts in millions

capital expenditures. When financing markets freeze up as they did during the fall of 2008, this potentially puts a greater strain on MLPs with near term funding needs. Management teams in those circumstances were faced with whether to pay out the cash flow they generate from operations (less maintenance capital expenditures), or cut the distribution in order to retain cash to continue funding growth projects.

Enterprise Value (EV)/Earnings Before Interest, Taxes, Depreciation and Amortization (EBITDA)

While typically a banking measure, investors use EV/EBITDA to understand both the relationship between the partnership as a whole (debt and equity) to its cash flow (EBITDA used as a proxy in this case), and further, to what a potential acquirer would pay in a sale transaction. This has become more relevant during this period of bifurcation as investors watch weaker MLPs' EV/EBITDA ratios to see if they get to a "sweet spot" where a stronger MLP might purchase them. Conversely, a higher EV/EBITDA means that the partnership units are likely to trade at a market premium and management may be more likely to engage as an acquirer in Mergers and Acquisitions (M&A) transactions by swapping their more expensive units for cheaper units of the target.

Net Income

Net income and net income per partnership unit are both measures disclosed by MLPs at reporting period intervals but both are less useful measures. The first reason is because of the role of depreciation. Depreciation charges are high due to the capital asset intensity of MLPs which leads to wide variances between net income and the partnership's true cash flow. Secondly, since MLPs are pass through tax entities and are subject to very little or no taxes (any taxes are typically levied at the state level), they bear little relationship to a C-Corp's reporting of net income. For these two reasons, investors focus on yield, distributable cash flow, and EBITDA as they are better measures of partnership cash flows and the amount of cash that an investor can expect to receive back from an MLP.

CASE STUDY: PLAINS ALL AMERICAN PIPELINES, LP

Plains All American Pipeline, LP (NYSE: PAA) is a publicly traded MLP engaged in the transportation, storage, terminaling and marketing of crude oil, refined products, and liquefied petroleum gas (LPG). The Partnership is also engaged in the development and operation of natural gas storage facilities.

PAA owns and operates a diversified portfolio of strategically located assets that play a vital role in the movement of United States and Canadian energy supplies. On average, they handle over 3 million barrels per day of crude oil, refined products and LPG through its extensive network of assets located in key North American producing basins and transportation gateways. PAA is headquartered in Houston, Texas. PAA's Valuation Summary as of June 30, 2009 is in Exhibit 6.9.

Dividend Discount Model

Some investors use the dividend discount model (DDM), also known as the Gordon Growth Model, to determine the equity value of partnership units.

EXHIBIT 6.9 Plains All American Pipeline Valuation Statement, June 2009

Price	$42.55		
Market Cap	5,319*		
Enterprise Value (EV)	9,137*		
Current quarterly distribution	$0.905		
Annualized distribution	$3.62	Current Yield	8.51%
2009 Distributable cash flow[1]	$4.16	Price/DCF	10.2x
2009 EBITDA[2]	977*	EV/EBITDA	9.4x

Notes:
[1] Broker consensus
[2] Midpoint of partnership guidance
*Dollar amounts in millions

This formula is expressed as:

$$Equity = \left(\frac{dividend}{rate - growth} \right) \text{ or } Equity = \left(\frac{D}{r - G} \right)$$

where *rate* is the required rate of return and *growth* is the growth rate of the dividend in perpetuity.

For PAA, using a $3.62 annual dividend, a 10.1 percent,[4] Weighted Average Cost of Capital (WACC) (the *r*), and a 3.4 percent growth rate, which is the 2009 full-year estimated distribution ($3.66) divided by 2008's full-year distribution ($3.54), the DDM suggests an equity value of $53.95.

$$EquityValue = \left(\frac{\$3.62}{10.1\% - 3.4\%} \right) = \$53.95$$

Of course, this presumes a constant WACC, and more important, a constant growth rate. If we take the long-term growth rate to 0, we arrive at an equity price of that is lower than the current market price by 18.5 percent.

$$EquityValue = \left(\frac{\$3.62}{10.1\% - 0.0\%} \right) = \$35.84$$

Alternatively, we can solve for the growth rate using the price of $42.55, which tells us that the market is implying a long-term growth rate of dividends of 1.87 percent:

$$\$44 = \left(\frac{\$3.62}{10.1\% - x\%} \right); \ x = 1.87\%$$

An investor, therefore, looking at PAA, assuming a 10.1 percent WACC, and desiring to buy or hold shares at $42.55 must decide if their view for distribution growth is higher than 1.87 percent long-term and by how much.

Distribution Discount Model

Another way that investors seek to value MLPs is by employing the concepts of a discounted cash flow model to MLPs distributable cash over a five-year period and discounting those cash flows to present value.

In this presentation, we'll still be relying on assumptions, but taking a cleaner look at distributions over the next five years. The assumptions are as follows (see Exhibit 6.10):

EXHIBIT 6.10   Drivers for Distribution
Discount Model

WACC	10.1%
2 yr implied	4.1%
Remaining 3 yr	3.5%
5 yr CAGR	3.7%
Terminal G	1.9%

Examining the Distribution Discount Model for PAA

- "WACC" as presented by PAA on June 10, 2009
- "2 yr implied" is the 2-year implied growth rate in distributable cash flow using Wall Street research analysts' consensus estimates
- "Remaining 3 yr" is the assumed, remaining 3-year growth rate
- "5 yr CAGR" is the 5-year compounded annual growth rate (CAGR) and is a function of the "2 yr implied" and "remaining 3 yr" growth rates
- The "Terminal G" is the terminal growth rate. In this instance, we took the 1.9 percent implied growth rate at $44 from the Gordon Growth approach.

Then we look at the present value from two different approaches: the *classic approach*, which applies a terminal growth rate to the year 5 distribution, and the *multiple approach*, which takes the view of an acquirer by placing a multiple on the final year cash flow.

Here we use the above assumptions in Exhibit 6.11 as well as a 1.10 times coverage ratio going forward to get to the annual estimated distribution or "owner's" cash. It should be noted that the $3.78 is higher than the 2009 estimated distribution of $3.62, but the difference in total equity value arising from this discrepancy is only $0.17.

Here we use the same assumptions in Exhibit 6.12 and results as before but we cap the terminal value at a multiple of 10.0 times assuming this is, conservatively, the most an acquirer would pay at a sale. It's also conservative since distribution/unit is typically much lower than EBITDA/unit (distribution is after interest, miscellaneous taxes, and the General Partner (GP) take), which is what an acquirer would focus on.

And to not anchor one's assumptions on the outputs from their model, it is helpful to construct sensitivity tables around the WACC and the remaining 3-year growth rate—the two biggest variables—to see what valuation looks like, under both approaches, using different value drivers (see Exhibit 6.13).

EXHIBIT 6.11 Classic Approach to Value

Classic Approach

Year	12/31/2008	12/31/2009	12/31/2010	12/31/2011	12/31/2012	12/31/2013
Dist cash[1,2]	$3.91	$4.16	$4.22	$4.37	$4.52	$4.68
Coverage	1.10x	1.10x	1.10x	1.10x	1.10x	1.10x
Distribution	$3.54	$3.78	$3.84	$3.97	$4.11	$4.25
Growth		6.8%	1.4%	3.5%	3.5%	3.5%
DCF		$3.60	$3.32	$3.12	$2.93	$2.76
Sum of cash flows		$15.73				
Terminal value		$33.49				
Total equity value		$49.22				
Implied terminal multiple		12.2x				

Notes:
[1] Actual distributable cash in 2008
[2] Use Wall Street estimates for 2009 and 2010

EXHIBIT 6.12 Multiple Approach to Value

Multiple Approach Year	12/31/2008	12/31/2009	12/31/2010	12/31/2011	12/31/2012	12/31/2013
Distribution[1]	$3.54	$3.78	$3.84	$3.97	$4.11	$4.25
Growth		6.8%	1.4%	3.5%	3.5%	3.5%
DCF		$3.60	$3.32	$3.12	$2.93	$2.76
Sum of cash flows		$15.73				
Terminal multiple		10.0x				
Terminal value		$27.56				
Total equity value		$43.29				

[1]From classic approach

EXHIBIT 6.13 DCF Sensitivity Analysis

Assumptions

WACC	Floating
2 yr implied growth	4.1%
Rem 3 yr growth	Floating
Terminal growth	1.9%
Multiple (only in "multiple approach")	10x

Classic Approach

		Remaining 3-Year Growth Rate							
		0.0%	1.5%	3.0%	4.5%	6.0%	7.5%	9.0%	10.5%
WACC	8.0%	$64.71	$67.17	$69.70	$72.30	$74.97	$77.71	$80.53	$83.43
	8.5%	$60.30	$62.55	$64.87	$67.26	$69.71	$72.23	$74.82	$77.48
	9.0%	$56.50	$58.58	$60.73	$62.93	$65.20	$67.52	$69.91	$72.37
	9.5%	$53.20	$55.14	$57.13	$59.17	$61.27	$63.43	$65.65	$67.93
	10.0%	$50.31	$52.11	$53.97	$55.87	$57.83	$59.85	$61.91	$64.03
	10.5%	$47.75	$49.44	$51.18	$52.96	$54.79	$56.68	$58.61	$60.59
	11.0%	$45.48	$47.06	$48.69	$50.37	$52.09	$53.85	$55.67	$57.53
	11.5%	$43.44	$44.93	$46.46	$48.04	$49.66	$51.33	$53.04	$54.79
	12.0%	$41.60	$43.01	$44.46	$45.95	$47.48	$49.05	$50.66	$52.32
	12.5%	$39.93	$41.27	$42.64	$44.05	$45.50	$46.99	$48.51	$50.08
	13.0%	$38.42	$39.69	$40.99	$42.33	$43.70	$45.11	$46.56	$48.05
	13.5%	$37.03	$38.24	$39.48	$40.75	$42.06	$43.40	$44.78	$46.19
	14.0%	$35.76	$36.91	$38.09	$39.30	$40.55	$41.83	$43.14	$44.48

Multiple Approach

		Remaining 3-Year Growth Rate							
		0.0%	1.5%	3.0%	4.5%	6.0%	7.5%	9.0%	10.5%
WACC	8.0%	$46.28	$47.89	$49.55	$51.26	$53.01	$54.81	$56.66	$58.55
	8.5%	$45.70	$47.28	$48.92	$50.60	$52.32	$54.09	$55.91	$57.78
	9.0%	$45.12	$46.69	$48.30	$49.95	$51.65	$53.39	$55.18	$57.02
	9.5%	$44.56	$46.10	$47.69	$49.31	$50.98	$52.70	$54.46	$56.27
	10.0%	$44.02	$45.53	$47.09	$48.69	$50.34	$52.03	$53.76	$55.54
	10.5%	$43.48	$44.97	$46.50	$48.08	$49.70	$51.36	$53.07	$54.83
	11.0%	$42.95	$44.42	$45.93	$47.48	$49.08	$50.72	$52.40	$54.12
	11.5%	$42.43	$43.88	$45.37	$46.90	$48.47	$50.08	$51.74	$53.44
	12.0%	$41.93	$43.35	$44.82	$46.32	$47.87	$49.46	$51.09	$52.76
	12.5%	$41.43	$42.83	$44.28	$45.76	$47.28	$48.85	$50.45	$52.10
	13.0%	$40.94	$42.33	$43.75	$45.21	$46.71	$48.25	$49.83	$51.45
	13.5%	$40.47	$41.83	$43.23	$44.67	$46.14	$47.66	$49.22	$50.82
	14.0%	$40.00	$41.34	$42.72	$44.13	$45.59	$47.09	$48.62	$50.20

Asset Value Approach

While it's important for investors to frame valuation expectations around cash flows, they must not lose sight of the value of fixed asset valuations, whether it is from a replacement cost (premium or discount to book value) or from a strategic perspective.

Intangibles Analysis

Investors must also spend time doing analysis around the factors that make a company strong using elements of Michael Porter's "Five Forces" analysis. The most important factors (in no particular order) that investors should pay attention to are:

- Strength and depth of the management team
- Alignment of management and shareholder interests
- Competitive moats
- Geographic positioning
- Broader partnership strategy

Applying this analysis to PAA, it represents one of the strongest management teams whether in or out of the MLP space. The core management team has been together for more than 20 years and they have worked to build a "bench" of talent that is capable of stepping in to fill any departures.

Management is also greatly aligned with shareholder interests whether it is through their significant ownership of PAA units and general partner units as part of their compensation, or as stewards of shareholder capital. Speaking to the use of excess capital generated as well as capital raised, on the first quarter 2009 conference call, CEO Greg Armstrong said "If ... the [more positive] feel of the environment in the financial markets were to continue, I would say it would be a positive sign for future distribution growth. If it got much weaker, I think it is a positive sign for PAA to be able to use that liquidity to take advantage of [acquisition] opportunities."[5]

The "moat" around PAA's assets is deep and wide. They maintain a dominant storage position in the crude oil hub of Cushing, Oklahoma, are building a dominant oil position in the Gulf Coast delivery point of St. James, Louisiana, and are building the dominant natural gas storage hub at Pine Prairie, Louisiana which will serve as a receipt point for Haynesville Shale gas.

Additionally, all of their storage and terminaling assets are geographically connected through a series of crude and refined products pipelines across the United States and Canada. This gives them the opportunity to present customers with multiple delivery points for their product to achieve highest market rates.

Lastly, PAA's broader strategy is that of conservative managers of capital who have no need to access the capital markets for internal growth projects through 2010, and who have the experience and customer relationships to put in to place high-return projects that ultimately grow partnership distributions well into the future.

THE FUTURE

Long-Term Macro Supply/Demand

MLPs will continue to serve vital takeaway, gathering and processing capacity for new areas of gas and oil supply. As shown in Exhibit 6.14, new drilling techniques and technology advances led to the discovery and commercialization of numerous new gas shale plays starting in the late 1990s with the Barnett Shale in North Texas and leading to 2008s Haynesville Shale in North Louisiana representing, potentially, the largest U.S. natural gas field ever discovered at 200 trillion cubic feet (33 billion barrel of oil equivalent).[6]

First half 2009 natural gas fundamentals reflects the commercialization of these new shale plays as a greater amount of gas coming out of the wells at higher initial production (IP) rates placed an oversupply of gas into a recessionary environment. This has caused the price of gas to drop from a high in July 2008 of $11.96/(1000 Cubic Feet)Mcf to the April 2009 low of $3.51/Mcf. But halfway through 2009, fundamentals appear to be slowly aligning as the number of natural gas rigs are down 55 percent from the end of June 2008 to end of June 2009 in response to low prices.

Short-term macro fundamentals aside, MLPs will benefit long term in conjunction with the EIA's projected U.S. energy demand growth. MLPs have the opportunity to construct new pipelines and storage in the highest growth areas of the country where demand is greater than the national average. MLPs also have the opportunity to participate in greater ethanol handling and transportation, as well as other opportunities that have been designated as qualified assets but not yet reached commercial viability such as clean coal, biodiesel, liquid hydrogen, liquid biomass, and liquid natural gas (LNG). Even looking further out there will be opportunities in other areas that have expressed interest such as solar, wind, and electric transmission industries.

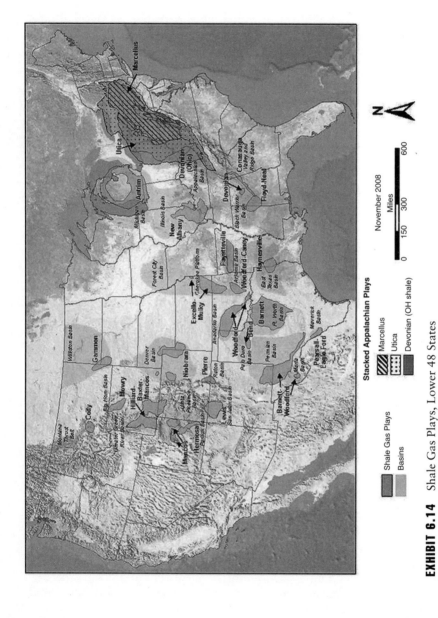

EXHIBIT 6.14 Shale Gas Plays, Lower 48 States

Source: Energy Information Administration, www.eia.doe.gov/pub/oil_gas/natural_gas/analysis.publications/maps/maps.html.

Distributions

Distribution growth should follow energy demand trends. Historical distribution growth has been approximately 5 percent versus the aforementioned 1980 to 2007 demand of 1.5 percent, and there appears nothing imminent that would change this historical pattern of distribution growth other than, of course, some annual dispersions around the mean.

One change which began in 2009 that is expected to continue is the realignment of the general partners' interests to be more in line with the limited partners' thereby increasing cash available to LP unit holders. Thus far in 2009, we've seen:

- Magellan Midstream Partners (NYSE: MMP) offers to buy in its general partner, Magellan Midstream Holdings (NYSE: MGG), thus eliminating future incentive distribution rights (IDRs) and lowering MMP's cost of capital.
- TransCanada Corp (NYSE: TRP), the general partner of TC Pipelines (NASDAQ: TCLP), agrees to reset its current IDRs from 50 percent of incremental cash flow to 2 percent with future IDRs capped at 25 percent. Similar to MMP, this lowers TCLP's cost of capital and allows it to be a more effective acquirer of assets from either TRP or third-party sellers.
- Williams Companies (NYSE: WMB) suspends its IDRs for Williams Partners (NYSE: WPZ) for all of 2009 to assist WPZ in covering its distribution in the low commodity price environment.
- The general partner of Plains All American (NYSE: PAA) temporarily suspends the IDRs on the cash flow associated with recent acquisition of its remaining 50 percent interest in the PAA/Vulcan Natural Gas Storage joint venture. This however is not without precedent. PAA's general partner similarly suspended the IDRs temporarily on cash flow associated with the 2008 acquisition of Rainbow Pipeline.

There is also a chance that new MLPs deciding to come to the public markets will have an LLC structure rather than a General Partner (GP)/Limited Partner (LP) structure. By choosing this course, there is no GP in place and therefore all cash flows come to unit holders proportionally. The LLC structure is currently in use for both Copano Energy (NYSE: CPNO) and Linn Energy (NYSE: LINE).

One final, emerging theme is the possibility that E&P MLPs could move away from a steady distribution model which encompasses very detailed and effective hedging schedules to a "pay what you earn" model that allows distributions to float more in line with commodity prices while still layering in some degree of hedging.

Capital Structures

Recent management commentary suggests MLPs will continue to target 50/50 debt/equity capital structures but that most will seek to manage their leverage (as measured by debt to EBITDA) toward the lower end of the 3.0 times to 4.0 times historical range, or even lower.

For noninvestment grade MLPs the picture is more complex. For those MLPs that have relied heavily on their revolving line of credit in order to finance the debt portion of their capital expenditures and acquisitions, they could face lower availability from their bank groups in 2011 and 2012 when the majority of facility terms expire. These MLPs may be forced to access the debt capital markets at higher rates than they are paying on their current revolvers due to both their noninvestment grade status, and higher amount of leverage. Their cost of capital should rise in conjunction with higher debt rates, making it difficult to fund growth initiatives. In addition, this may put pressure on their ability to sustain distributions at current quarterly payout rates.

Changing Characteristics of MLPs

In the intermediate term, it is possible that the total number of MLPs will be lower than present. This could happen through mergers and acquisitions, as the stronger partnerships acquire the weaker ones, and through some partnership dissolutions arising from technical default due to failed business models caused by poorly managed capital structures. In 2009, there have been five proposed M&A transactions, which would reduce the total number to 73 from 78 (see Exhibit 6.15).

EXHIBIT 6.15 Proposed MLP M&A Transactions in 2009

Date Announced	Acquirer	Ticker	Target	Ticker
3/3/2009	Harold Hamm	Private	Hiland Partners LP	HLND
3/3/2009	Harold Hamm	Private	Hiland Holdings GP, LP	HPGP
3/3/2009	Magellan Midstream Ptrs	MMP	Magellan Midstream Hldgs	MGG
4/3/2009	Apollo Mgt	Private	Legacy Resources	LGCY
4/27/2009	Atlas America	ATLS	Atlas Energy Resources	ATN
6/29/2009	Enterprise Prod Ptrs	EPD	TEPPCO Ptrs	TPP

In addition to changes caused by potential M&A activity, gatherer and processors are motivated to restructure certain of their contracts. It is likely that the gathering and processing segment as a whole will lessen their exposure to contracts tied to equity volumes, which are much more sensitive to the price of commodities, and towards having a stronger percentage of fixed fee contracts. This will reduce the volatility of cash flows, decrease the need for extensive and expensive hedging programs, and provide a more stable stream of cash flow. Over a longer period of time, it is expected that the total number of publicly traded MLPs will be greater as either new partnerships will be brought public to meet existing energy infrastructure demand, or they will take advantage of the opportunities in emerging energy trends that have qualified for MLP status.

Future for MLP Ownership

Institutional investors are becoming keenly aware of the value proposition that MLPs offer. MLPs have historically traded with yields of 6 percent to 7 percent and delivered growth of 4 percent to 8 percent due to the combination of organic growth from new projects, contract escalators, and GDP oriented energy demand growth of 1.5 percent per annum. Because of these factors, MLPs' total return profile has historically averaged in the low to mid teens. MLPs offer a compelling total return profile for investors considering infrastructure investments. They have modest risk attributes, complete transparency and liquidity through public markets, low correlation with other asset classes, and little to no political or labor risk.

The future institutional use of MLPs will nevertheless hinge on a few important factors. Education and knowledge of the investment attributes will propel institutional ownership higher from its approximate 25 percent current ownership rate. Market capitalization and liquidity will continue to grow and improve, giving institutional investors the visibility and transparency they require when assessing the legitimacy of an emerging asset class. Importantly, MLPs have breached the $100 billion equity market cap threshold. Once an institutional investor decides to make an MLP allocation, they must formulate allocation strategies that properly reflect which "bucket" MLPs belong. It is likely that due to the flexible investment attributes that MLPs bring to bear, there could be a wide variety of outcomes as to which asset class an MLP allocation would fit. Determining the asset class with the best fit would ultimately depend on the investment structure, characteristics, and the objectives of the institutional investor's portfolio. MLPs have found their way into allocations for real assets, high income allocations, inflation hedging allocations, and infrastructure allocations.

MLPs are certain to find meaningful and useful allocations within institutional portfolios. The ground swell of institutional interest has just begun and MLPs are expected to ride a trajectory of asset growth. With their compelling attributes, MLPs deserve to be considered as a core holding in any infrastructure allocation.

ENDNOTES

1. Energy Information Administration, "Annual Energy Outlook 2009 With Projections to 2030." Energy Information Administration, March 2009. www.eia.doe.gov/oiaf/aeo/demand.html.
2. International Business Times, "Clean Coal Infrastructure in U.S. Estimated to Cost $1 Trillion: Experts." *International Business Times*, April 27, 2009. www.ibtimes.com/articles/20090427/clean-coal-infrastructure-ins-estimated-costtrillion.htm.
3. Kinder Morgan Energy Partners, L.P., "Company Presentation." (UBS 2009 MLP Conference, June 3-4, 2009).
4. Plains All American Pipeline, L.P. "PAA: Tested. Delivered. Positioned." (2009 PAA Analyst Meeting Presentation June 10, 2009).
5. Armstrong, Greg L., "Plains All American Pipeline, L.P. First Quarter Results 2009 Conference Call." May 7, 2009.
6. Casselman, Ben, "U.S. Gas Fields Go From Boom to Bust," *Wall Street Journal*, April 30, 2009, A1. http://online.wsj.com/article/SB124104549891270585.html.

CHAPTER 7

Clean Energy Infrastructure

Moving from a Niche Opportunity to a Mainstream Asset Class

Scott Lawrence
Investment Director, Fortis Investments

Peter Dickson
Technical Director, Fortis Investments

DEFINING CLEAN ENERGY INFRASTRUCTURE

The world of renewable energy investment is vast with many different asset classes, investment vehicles, technologies, risk/reward trade-offs, return profiles, and market participants. There are publicly listed equities that allow access to renewable energy exposure in terms of technology producers and electrical utility companies, among others. There is venture capital, which allows investors to gain exposure to new and unproven technologies such as electricity storage devices attached to wind turbines. Private equity plays its part in terms of expansion capital funding for existing companies that want to increase production capacity or enter new marketplaces. Some investment classes allow focused access to renewable energy only, and others allow access as part of a larger portfolio of opportunities. The combination of all these sectors that make up renewable energy investment has increased an industry that is large and is growing quickly with the year 2008 seeing a global spend of $155 billion (USD).[1]

For the purposes of this chapter, the investment class examined will be renewable energy infrastructure, specifically electricity generation on a utility scale through clean and renewable means. The following descriptions detail the most common technologies that are installed.

Wind. Normally a three-bladed horizontal-axis turbine constructed on a high tower that is either land based or offshore. Wind turbines vary in capacity but can generate as much as 5MW. The key value drivers for wind energy are the blade area of the turbine and the velocity of wind coming across the blades. Location is vital as a constant supply of strong wind is necessary to make the asset profitable.

Solar Photovoltaic (PV). Solar panels are made from a thin layer of semiconducting material (usually silicon) and create energy when photons from the sun strike the panel and create a DC electrical current. PV has been one of the more capital-intensive technologies, but the recent past has seen prices coming down significantly. The future of PV is promising due to this continued price decrease, the technologies being a good match to the power demand curve, and its relative ease of installation.

Biomass. Similar to traditional fossil fuel combustion-based power plants, but different in that the fuel used is derived directly from trees, plants, and other organic material. The main driver for a biomass power plant is the calorific value of materials being burned and the consistent sourcing of material used (usually through long-term supply contracts). Biomass plants operate by either burning solid biomass directly or through the creation of gaseous fuels from the underlying biomass.

Small Hydro. Generally defined as hydroelectric plants with capacity less than 30MW. Projects are usually run-of-the-river schemes in which the natural flow of water is used to generate power, rather than induced flow under pressure from a dam. Key value drivers for this technology are the consistent flow of water and strong water velocity.

Geothermal. Geothermal energy is sourced from the heat contained within the earth. This technology is generally used to exploit hot underground water that has reached the surface or which can be acquired by drilling boreholes.

The reason that these technologies are the most commonly installed is that they are considered proven within the renewable energy infrastructure investment community. Moderately long operational track records exist for these technologies and risk of nonperformance is considered low. Other technologies such as concentrating solar power, tidal, wave, and others are also considered in the renewable energy power generation space, but the installed base is not as high and certain issues must be dealt with to allow them to be more mainstream in the future.

RENEWABLE ENERGY IN EUROPE

This chapter examines the implementation of these electricity generation technologies in a European context because Europe remains the global leader in terms of renewable energy infrastructure (http://sefi.unep.org/fileadmin/media/sefi/docs/publications/UNEP_SEFI_Global_Trends_Report_2009_f.pdf, section 1.3). Europe enjoys this leading position due to its early adoption for the reasons of climate change, growing power demand, energy security, and more recently as a job growth mechanism. As shown in Exhibit 7.1, European states have implemented long-term transparent legislation that adequately supports the construction of these power plants. As a result of this legislation and experience set, Europe currently accounts for 49.7 percent of net new investment in the renewable energy space (http://sefi.unep.org/fileadmin/media/sefi/docs/publications/UNEP_SEFI_Global_Trends_Report_2009_f.pdf, figure 13).

The United States, China, India, among others, are increasing efforts and support for renewable energy electricity generation. Growth rates for

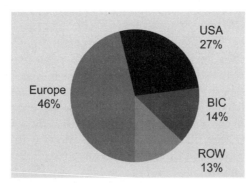

EXHIBIT 7.1   New Investment in Renewable Energy by Region

Notes: BIC: Brazil, India, China
ROW: Rest of World
Source: Fortis Clean Energy Fund and United Nations Environment Program, June 2008.

the industry outside of Europe are promising, further moving the industry into the mainstream of the investment world. However, Europe is likely to hold its dominant position for the next several years.

GENESIS AND GROWTH OF CLEAN ENERGY INFRASTRUCTURE

Historical Developments

The early interest in renewable energy development was created not by concern over perceived environmental damage by fossil fuel usage, but by concern over energy security. During the 1970s oil crisis, the developed world was made to realize how exposed it was to insecurity in hydrocarbon supplies from a small number of oil producing nations. From the beginning of the oil embargo in October 1973, to the beginning of hostilities in the Iran-Iraq war in 1981, the price of a barrel of imported crude oil rose by about 13 times in nominal terms.

Throughout the 1970s, a number of initiatives ran parallel and looked at educational, commercial, and regulatory programs for the promotion of wind as an alternative source of energy. By the end of the decade, wind was being used to produce private sources of power on a large scale particularly in California.

In the 1980s, a period of stability returned to oil prices that had the effect of slowing down progress in U.S. alternative energy development; however, by the end of the 1970s, Europe had already picked up the baton and was working toward the commercialization of wind power generation. In 1978, the British Wind Energy Association was launched, creating a means through which scientists and development organizations would collaborate. In 1982, the European Wind Energy Association was inaugurated, originally as a trade association supporting those European manufacturers that were exporting turbines and other equipment to California as part of the "Californian wind rush." These organizations, along with their equivalents in other European States, encouraged and nurtured an emerging European renewable energy industry.

Much of the interest in renewable power generation during this period was focused on creating the opportunities for sustainable development in developing nations. Renewable energy offered an alternative to imported fossil fuels for many countries who were struggling to support their populations and to industrialize. As a consequence, much of the focus was on off-grid systems primarily for rural electrification. Hydroelectric power, the first mover in utility scale power generation, reduced in scale to adapt to the needs of remote communities. Small-scale (up to about 30MW), micro-scale (up to approximately 1MW), and finally pico-scale generation (up to 1kW) were perfected for community use. Solar photovoltaic technology also became a useful, albeit expensive, source of remote power. Wind power did not largely benefit from this period of development due to its unpredictability as a stand-alone source of power.

In 1991, oil prices peaked as a consequence of the first Gulf War. Minds once again became focused on the sensitivity of the exposure Western-developed countries had to relatively unstable oil-producing countries. This time the increased awareness of energy security coincided with another looming issue; that of increased concern over environmental damage from fossil fuel emissions and man-made climate change.

Climate Change

Concern grew throughout the 1990s that the recent recorded warming of the atmosphere was a function of the levels of CO_2 in the atmosphere. This concern grew among environmentalists and came to the forefront of policy of governments in both Europe and the United States. In 1992, the "Earth Summit" was held in Rio de Janiero, where the United Nations Framework Convention on Climate Change (UNFCCC) was initiated. The UNFCCC began a process of negotiation of the reduction of so-called greenhouse gases, which continued with the 3rd Conference of the Parties (COP3) at Kyoto in 1997 where the Kyoto Protocol was agreed. The Protocol created binding targets for the reduction of greenhouse gases and formed the backdrop for the development of subsequent measures globally for the promotion of sustainability, including in the energy sphere.

The Kyoto Protocol came into force in November 2004, when Russia's ratification saw the achievement of countries representing no less than 55 percent of the world's 1990 equivalent CO_2 emissions having ratified the treaty. Since that date, an increasing number of countries have taken steps to reduce carbon emissions from their industrial sectors, much of which is created by energy generation.

Decentralization of Generation

Early electrification programs focused on decentralized "island-mode" power communities with limited transmission of power. Such networks were driven by relatively small power stations, with lower thermal efficiency than today's large centralized stations. In the second half of the 20th century, a trend existed toward centralization of generation close to the point of production of fuel. Large thermally efficient power stations were created close to centers of fuel production and power was delivered to the consumer through large networks of transmission and distribution.

Current trends are toward distribution of generation around the transmission networks, reducing transport losses, and enhancing security of delivery by reducing the requirement for transmission. This trend is most clearly seen in Europe, where now the Netherlands, Finland, and Denmark each produce more than 40 percent of their current generation from decentralized plants.[2]

In this context, renewable energy is often an appropriate form of power generation, utilizing smaller sources of power distributed around the network, close to many centers of demand.

Energy Security

In recent years, the issue of energy security has once again become acute. The energy crisis of the 1970s raised concerns about the sourcing of energy from politically sensitive regions and recent trends have further exacerbated these fears. Europe's falling known oil and gas reserves and its consequential increasing dependence on imported hydrocarbons demonstrate the validity of concerns. Northern Europe is becoming increasingly dependent on gas imported from Russia through the Baltic pipelines; Southern Europe uses gas from the Caspian gas fields imported through the Caucasus. Both these routes are subject to a number of politically sensitive regions. The cutting of Russian supplies of gas to Ukraine in the winter of 2006 and again in the winter of 2008, and on a smaller scale, the cutting of Uzbek gas to Kyrgyzstan in response to a dispute over refugees show clearly how energy can become a point of political leverage.

Europe suffers from exposure to all of these issues: sensitivity to climate change, a drive toward decentralization of power, and a growing dependence on imported energy put Europe at the forefront of the development of renewable energy worldwide.

THE EUROPEAN RENEWABLES DIRECTIVE

In 1997, a White Paper was produced in Europe that defined subsequent European policy for the promotion of renewable energy. The subsequent directive, The Directive on the Promotion of Electricity from Renewable Energy Sources in the Internal Electricity Market (the Renewables Directive) was adopted in 2001. This established an overall target for the proportion of electricity that each member state should procure from renewable sources. It established a market that has lead global developments in renewable energy ever since.

In response to the Renewables Directive, member states each adopted a national target for renewable power generation. The targets were dependent on natural resources, current carbon emissions, and the structure of the national power market. Targets vary greatly across Europe, from 10 percent in Malta to 49 percent in Sweden due to its historic use of renewables as a source of power. For the calculation of existing capacity, large hydroelectric generation is counted as renewable, but is excluded from future stimulus packages, due to its commercial viability without support.

In 2008, a revision to the Renewables Directive was adopted, which established the 20:20:20 paradigm, that by 2020, 20 percent of Europe's total energy demand will be sourced from renewable sources. In this case, energy refers to all forms of energy usage: transport, heat, and electricity. As heat and transport fuels present a number of problems to achieve the target, it is widely anticipated that the electricity sector will carry the lion's share of the burden.

The Renewables Directive identifies targets for total energy from renewables in each member state and requires each to publish a detailed national plan for how this will be achieved, by December 2009. At this time, it is anticipated that the existing targets for the renewable share of electricity markets will be significantly increased. In the meantime, the current targets are shown in Exhibit 7.2.

The implementation of a new directive is to be monitored closely by the European Commission. In 2011, each member state must present a report on progress toward national targets, and subsequent reports at least two-year intervals thereafter.

In order to achieve the targets imposed, each member state has adopted a mechanism for the promotion of renewable energy development. These mechanisms have evolved over time but in general they all utilize one or more of the following five elements:

Feed-In Tariffs. Feed-in tariffs provide a pricing structure for power produced from renewable energy installations, in which power supply companies must purchase renewable energy from compliant generation plants at a defined price for a defined period of time. The feed-in tariff removes all volume and pricing risk for the developer and investor to the project and has emerged as the most common of the stimulus systems in Europe, and arguably the most popular with investors for its mitigation of risk.

EXHIBIT 7.2 Existing and Target Share of Energy from Renewable Sources: 2005–2020

	National overall targets for share of energy from renewable sources in final consumption of energy, 2005	Target for share of energy from renewable sources in final consumption of energy, 2020
Belgium	2.2%	13%
Bulgaria	9.4	16
The Czech Republic	6.1	13
Denmark	17.0	30
Germany	5.8	18
Estonia	18.0	25
Ireland	3.1	16
Greece	6.9	18
Spain	8.7	20
France	10.3	23
Italy	5.2	17
Cyprus	2.9	13
Latvia	34.9	42
Lithuania	15.0	23
Luxembourg	0.9	11
Hungary	4.3	13
Malta	0.0	10
The Netherlands	2.4	14
Austria	23.3	34
Poland	7.2	15
Portugal	20.5	31
Romania	17.8	24
Slovenia	16.0	25
The Slovak Republic	6.7	14
Finland	28.5	38
Sweden	39.8	49
United Kingdom	1.3	15

Source: European Commission, 2005.

Quota Obligations. Also known as Renewable Portfolio Standards or Certificate Systems, this element imposes an obligation on electricity suppliers to source a defined proportion of their power from renewable sources. In order to incentivize the generation of renewable power, a market for certificates is created in which certificates are sold by the generator to the power supplier in order to demonstrate compliance with the obligation. The operation of the market encourages efficiency in the system and ensures best value for money, while the market risk implied is balanced by the higher value of the certificates relative to feed-in tariffs. While feed-in tariffs are most common across Europe, a number of countries use Certificate Systems, for instance the United Kingdom, Sweden, and Poland.

Tariff Tendering. In the early days of the development of regulation, tendering systems for the identification of tariffs were used by a number of countries. In the United Kingdome for instance, the Non-Fossil Fuel Obligation (NFFO) operated through a series of calls for projects, where developers placed bids for tariffs based on the anticipated performance of plant. The system has largely been abandoned, after a high failure rate among projects awarded with tariffs.

Capital Grant. Capital grants are frequently used as a mechanism for the support of technologies in development, but rarely for more commercially proven technologies.

Fiscal Measures. A number of fiscal measures are in use in Europe and other countries. Incentives to invest in energy efficient and renewable energy plants include accelerated depreciation of capital items and enhanced allowances for renewables. Very often fiscal measures are used in conjunction with other mechanisms.

FUTURE GROWTH

It is clear that the market for renewable energy in Europe is mature and stable. There is a significant amount of experience among all actors in the industry, from regulators and operators to developers and financiers. The European market has grown steadily over the past 10 years, and the new targets ensure that growth will continue for the foreseeable future.

The European Wind Energy Association (EWEA) anticipates that massive growth will occur in the next 12 years. Christian Kjaer, EWEA chief executive, said "The target implies that renewable energy's share of electricity will increase from 15% today to more than a third of Europe's demand in 2020. Wind energy will be the biggest contributor to that massive increase in clean electricity production."[3]

Each year, the United Nations Environment Program, in conjunction with the Sustainable Energy Finance initiative and New Energy Finance, produce their reports on global trends in sustainable energy financing. The 2009 report shows that in 2008 financing of renewable energy assets grew by 12.9 percent to $116.9 billion, and that $49.7 billion of this was invested in European assets.

With future growth ensured by mandatory targets, demand for capital will be great. In the past, growth could be financed by utilities and other strategic investors alone, but with multiple demands on their capital and because of the sheer capacity of generation assets to be developed, alternative sources of finance are required. This has led to the emergence of the financial investor with increasing numbers of transactions being done with this source of private equity capital. The emergence of these financial players has enabled a robust market for renewable energy power plants to develop thereby increasing appetite for new construction. This trend appears to be positive as increasingly new financial players enter the renewable energy infrastructure market space every year.

Limitations

While the policy and regulatory backdrop remain positive, logistical limits exist to the unfettered expansion of renewable energy. Most forms of renewables are directly responsive to natural resources and phenomena and are therefore intermittent and variable by nature. A national electricity grid needs to be responsive to the needs of fluctuating demand and able to be built up and cut back accordingly. Unschedulable renewable capacity therefore must be balanced by more flexible schedulable sources of power. While the practical limit this places on the proportion of renewables on a network remains the subject of debate, it is probably somewhere between 15 percent and 20 percent. Denmark has the highest proportion of wind power of any country in the world, with 19.7 percent of the national power consumption coming from wind power in 2007.[4] Although this figure has fallen slightly in the last two years, it establishes a precedent that allows a much greater proportion of Europe's power to be planned from wind power than previously thought.

Practical limits to the development of renewables are based on limitations on the use of land, potential to access consent, and access to distribution and transmission grids. For the time being, until network limits are approached, the efficiency of the development process itself is the key to the successful deployment of renewable sources of energy in the European Union.

DEAL STRUCTURE

Understanding the drivers and evolution of the renewable energy infrastructure space in Europe, it is time to move into the actual creation of power plants on the ground. This section begins with the development process and finishes with a case study to further clarify the process.

Overview of the Development Process

The development of a renewable energy power plant can be best illustrated through a three-step process. Each stage of the process has different participants, as well as difference risk–reward characteristics. (See Exhibit 7.3.)

Development Phase   The development phase is the most complicated stage of the development process and generally is the territory of specialist development companies. These companies range in size from a few individuals with exceptionally strong local connections, to larger organizations with over 100 members of staff. The developer will form a company called a special purpose vehicle (SPV) that will hold all the project rights. The work involved includes buying/leasing a land parcel, performing power plant yield analysis, environmental impact assessments, zoning changes, construction permits, grid interconnection plan, and the all-important power purchase agreement (PPA) signed with a regional utility company. It is not until the developer has finished their work that construction can begin.

Construction Phase   The time when the development phase ends and the construction phase begins is often referred to as financial close. Financial

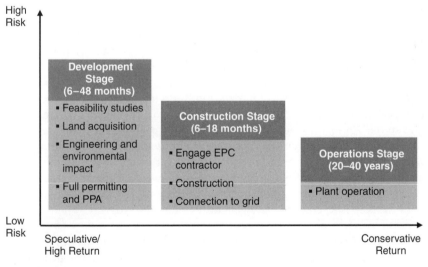

EXHIBIT 7.3   Development Process of Renewable Energy Power Plants

close is the point at which the developer has successfully brought the project through the development phase, and the follow-on equity investor can take control of the SPV, raise project finance (debt), and sign the construction contracts. The SPV and the leases, contracts, and permits it holds are subject to a detailed due diligence process by the follow-on-equity investor. If there is to be project finance on the power plant, the lender will also conduct a thorough due diligence study.

Construction is performed by specialist construction companies within the renewable energy industry. In general, there are two types of construction contract structures. One is the turnkey contract. This is a situation when the equity investor signs a single engineer, procure, and construct (EPC) contract with a single company. This EPC contract is referred to as *turnkey* because the EPC contractor is completely responsible for the power plant design, procurement of the necessary equipment, the civil works necessary on the land parcel, and the full construction of the power plant. A bit of a simplification, but this essentially means that the equity investor signs the EPC contract and is delivered an operational power plant.

To mitigate the risks the investors takes through the construction phase, turnkey EPC contracts are structured with a strong collection of guarantees and warranties. These generally focus on the power plant being delivered on time and at the correct specifications. Failure to do so invokes penalties against the EPC contractor that include the investors withholding payments and potential refunds to the investors. Due to the importance of these guarantees and warranties, the credit quality of the EPC contractor must be examined to ensure they have both the willingness and ability to pay on any penalty due.

The second type of construction contract structure is multicontracting. In this situation, the equity owner will spread the construction responsibilities among several companies. The construction process of the power plant can have several moving pieces including providers for engineering services, civil works, electrical integration, sourcing of the power generation unit (i.e., a wind turbine), cabling, invertors, transformers, concrete, steel, and so on. An investor might choose to go this path for economic reasons, or because a full turnkey EPC contract is not available. The advantages to the multicontracting approach are cost savings (through transparent pricing and margin reduction) and greater control. However, project management becomes more time consuming and the guarantees and warranties associated with turnkey EPC contracts are generally not as robust.

Operations Phase   Once a renewable energy power plant passes through the construction phase, it then commences operations and starts producing electricity. This electricity is generally sold to a utility company or grid operator under the economic terms of a PPA discussed in previous sections (i.e., feed-in tariffs, certificates, etc.).

It is at this stage that the power plant is considered significantly de-risked as there is no further development or construction risk. The main risk at this stage is operational risk, and can be controlled through the use of an operations and maintenance (O&M) contract. The O&M contract provides for ongoing operations and periodic maintenance of a renewable energy power plant, and is often signed with the EPC contractor due to their technical expertise and knowledge of the asset. O&M contracts are of varying duration, and come with certain operational guarantees that vary depending on technology and geography.

Beyond the cost of the O&M contract, the project is subject to charges for the land lease, insurance, taxes, debt service on the project finance, and some minor miscellaneous charges.

STRUCTURE OF FUNDING

Building on Balance Sheet

The construction of renewable energy power plants is funded through a variety of means. Certain large investors in the space can construct a plant using only their balance sheets. These companies are often utility companies and can build these power plants with equity capital only as their internal cost of capital, as measured through their weighted cost of capital (WACC), is sufficiently below the returns generated from the plan.[5]

Other investors may choose to build on balance sheet for strategic reasons. An example of this would be a company that manufactures the underlying technology being used in the renewable energy power plant. These companies will build a plant with their own funds in order to demonstrate the technology's viability so that it can then be deemed as proven under normal operations.

Use of Project Finance

Other investors in renewable energy power plants make use of a combination of their own equity capital and nonrecourse project finance in the construction process. Project finance is a vital source of funding for most investors. See Exhibit 7.4.

Project finance is a long-term debt instrument provided by banks that specialize in lending against renewable energy power generation assets. These loans typically account for 40 percent to 90 percent of a power

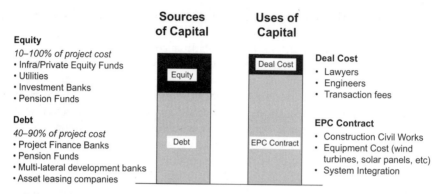

EXHIBIT 7.4   Sources of Capital and Uses of Capital

plant's cost depending on the technology used and project locations. Project finance loans are nonrecourse, meaning that the bank that has written the loan has recourse only to the renewable energy power plant itself in the event of default. Except in the case of fraud or gross misrepresentation, the equity investor normally has no further losses beyond their initial investment in the plant. This risk sharing of the plant's performance means that the due diligence process performed by the bank that lends to an asset is detailed and rigorous.

Debt terms range in length from 5 to 25 years depending on the type, location, and support mechanism for the renewable energy power plant. Generally speaking, wind and solar PV assets are allowed terms of 15 to 20 years, reflecting the robustness of the technologies and the long-term clarity in the power plant's returns. Pricing, fees, and covenants required by the lending banks vary depending on general market conditions, but having a fixed interest rate is very important as interest rate risk is of great concern in these assets due to relatively stable revenues that generally cannot grow faster than inflation. In other words, a power plant with floating rate interest on its project finance could go into default in a high interest rate environment.

CURRENT PROJECT FINANCE MARKET

As of this writing, lending banks are more conservative than they were in the recent past. The effects of the credit crunch have meant that banks have increased their pricing and are stricter in their underwriting.

An additional hurdle in today's project finance market is that borrowers cannot generally go to a single bank for a loan. In the recent past, this was much the norm as a single bank would lend the full amount of the loan, and then sell off or syndicate pieces of that loan to other banks. The credit crunch severely paired back the syndication market, thereby creating a situation in which project finance banks are currently only willing to fund a portion of the debt required for a project. This means that equity investors need to approach more than one bank and request that each will lend part of the loan. This is known as a *club deal*, and has meant that renewable energy projects typically require two to five banks to provide one project finance loan. For onshore wind projects, usually two to three banks as transaction sizes are more manageable.

Yet a further complication to these club deals is the domestically focused tendencies of the project finance banks in the current economy. These banks have a preference to lend in their own countries, or support projects in other countries that use the technology provided by domestic suppliers. In the European context, this appears to act as a support mechanism to the pricing of European goods in comparison to their Asian counterparts. For example, many European project finance banks will only loan to those solar projects that use European solar panels. Interestingly enough, European manufactured polycrystalline solar panels still command a premium over Asian panels for what is arguably the same quality product.

Despite the given difficulties in the project finance markets, renewable energy generation assets have the benefit of being smaller in size than other power generation assets, and have a strong government-based support mechanism for their revenues. For these reasons, project finance is still widely available in the marketplace. Transactions just happen to take longer.

CASE STUDY

Spanish Solar Photovoltaic Power Plant

An examination of a 1 MW[6] photovoltaic power plant in Spain gives one a tangible example to some of the elements in the previous sections.

Photovoltaic (PV) plants in Spain built prior to the end of September 2008 were subject to a law named Royal Decree (RD) 661/2007. Under RD 661/2007, a project would earn a feed-in tariff price of € 0.44 per kWh for 25 years with an annual inflation adjustment. Most polycrystalline-based PV panels come with a warranted degradation factor of 0.5 percent per year, ensuring that the output of the system is known so long as the level of solar irradiation is known (this number is widely available and does not fluctuate

EXHIBIT 7.5 Installation of Solar Modules
Source: Fortis Investments.

significantly over time). The product of the output in terms of kWh and the base pricing of € 0.44 per kWh yields the overall revenue of the power plant with a high degree of certainty. For a 1 MW power plant in the Spanish region of Murcia, this would be:

$$1,500,000 \text{ kWh} \times 0.44 \text{ €/kWh} = \text{€ } 660.000 \text{ per year}$$

This number has of course an annual inflation adjustment and would grow over the 25 year feed in tariff time horizon.

The ongoing costs for this power plant would include the operations and maintenance contract, land lease, insurance, accounting, filing, local taxes, and some other miscellaneous charges. These costs tend to be no more than 15 percent of revenues, giving this power plant a very high operating margin.

The rest of the financial model for this power plant would include the debt service to be paid on the project finance loan and Spanish corporate taxes. The net result would be a free cash flow to equity number over the life of the power plant. From here, return calculations on an internal rate of return (IRR) or net present value basis can be computed for deal pricing and subsequent investment decisions.

A power plant such as this one has a useful life of approximately 40 years, but the tariff in Spain ends after 25 years. Most investment cases are made on the life of the tariff length, but there is some residual value left after the 25-year period. Certainly, the power plant should be able to, at the termination of the feed-in tariff, sell into the grid at what is then the wholesale price for electricity production. Further, as the site has already been set aside for solar power, and the grid connection is in place, a future owner of the plant could choose to repower the site. This would entail pulling out the older less efficient panels that were used at the inception of the plant, and installing what one could assume to be a more cost and output efficient panel available in 25 years' time. (See Exhibit 7.5.)

Innovation Expected

Competition for limited resources and environmental concerns mean that we are in a period of uncertainty and change with respect to sources of energy. This is often portrayed as competition between alternative sources, such as nuclear energy versus renewables or centralized versus distributed. As the 21st-century energy paradigm develops, it is becoming apparent that there is not likely to be any one "winner" in the search for alternative sources of power, but a wide and diverse mix offering security though diversification and a reduction in use of fossil fuels. In fact, there has been work done that suggests that the addition of fixed-cost power generation technologies to a portfolio of conventional generating assets serves to reduce the overall cost of power to the consumer by the reduction of risk in the portfolio in general.[7]

The energy mix of Europe in the future is therefore likely to be a more diverse and distributed model than anything seen in the past. It also means that future technological developments are unlikely to be seen as replacements for the current generation mix, but rather as complementary to it.

Manufacturing Gains

In the interim, technological developments mean that energy planners have more tools at their disposal than ever before. The cost of conventional renewable energy devices is becoming continually cheaper, particularly in recent years solar photovoltaics. In 1993, the cost of an installed watt of PV power in Japan was on average 3750 yen[8] or $36.5 per watt (USD) in 1993. Since then, the industry has grown at a tremendous rate in terms of production capacity of traditional solar PV panels, and newer technologies such as thin film. An installed watt of the same type of solar PV installed in 1993 Japan would today cost $4.5 per watt in southern Europe.

Emerging Technologies

Renewable energy remains an emerging technological sector and while existing assets are secured for their useful life by the foresight of regulators, new innovation is constantly emerging. In the next decade, we can expect to see a number of innovations that offer exciting new opportunities for investors, whatever their risk appetite. The following is merely a sample of what innovations may be expected.

Solar Thermal Power

A number of pilot projects are currently under development for the construction of solar thermal power. The use of solar power to heat water and generate power in the steam cycle is simple and effective. In southern Europe and in North Africa, a number of projects are either operational or in development. An amount of interest has been generated in a proposal to develop large solar thermal power stations in North Africa to supply power to Europe. While this has undoubted value, it cannot address the full range of drivers for alternative power, such as the desire for energy independence or the reduction of losses though the distribution of generation throughout the transmission network. However, the promise of the technology is high as it has the potential to deliver fully schedulable power to the grid network through storage of excess heat in the system that can later be converted into electricity.

Reducing Cost of Wind Power

Wind power has similarly reduced greatly in price and now in a number of areas is approaching grid parity, the target price where the technology is considered to be able to compete with conventional source of power without subsidy. Wind is likely to continue to reduce in price as installations become larger. As a consequence, the latest progress in the development of offshore wind is creating an expectation of a step change in renewable energy cost toward grid parity.

Greater Use of Biomass

Biomass-based power generation differs from other renewables in that it relies on the overall cycle of elements used as energy carriers for its acceptance as renewable. That is, it is taken that the volume of carbon and other emissions from the biomass-fueled power station is exactly balanced by the volume of the same materials absorbed by the biomass fuel when it is growing. Therefore, over the duration of the growing cycle of the fuel, the system can be considered carbon- and other emissions-neutral. The shorter the growing cycle, the lesser the impact on the atmosphere.

The main value of biomass, however, is that unlike any other renewable energy technology, biomass is entirely schedulable and flexible. As Europe continues to develop larger and larger proportions of renewable energy capacity, so the need for more flexible capacity also grows. In recognition of biomass's flexibility, and in response to the limited land available for wind developments, the United Kingdom has adopted a highly favorable subsidy regime for biomass plants, with up to double subsidies being offered to the most efficient plant, or those utilizing innovative technologies.

Electricity Storage and Hydrogen

Future developments in energy will likely focus on allowing greater and greater capacity of renewable power to be developed, especially as prices drop. Technologies for the effective storage of electricity are prime among these developments. The biggest hurdle to the larger development of renewable power is its variability and the need for other sources of power for balancing. Fuel cell technology storing power and allowing it to be dispatched evenly would remove the upper limit, for example, to the deployment of wind power.

The most advanced fuel cell technologies are based on the use of hydrogen, which as yet cannot be produced on an industrial scale without the use itself of very large amounts of energy. Developments on the sustainable production of hydrogen will provide not only effective electricity storage but also the possibility of totally emissions-free transport fuel.

CONCLUSION

Renewable energy has matured significantly over the past five years. While it remains dependent on subsidies, the subsidies themselves are now underwritten by robust and secure policy that matches long-term developments in the power sector.

Europe especially has established itself as the leading innovator of regulation for alternative energy. Regulation developed in Europe is being followed by an increasing number of countries.

An investor with an appetite for steady, secure cash flow, well-managed risk, almost guaranteed market growth and a socially responsible element to their portfolio should seriously consider European renewable energy generation.

The drivers behind the shift to alternative energy are based on long-term issues that will serve to increase demand in the coming years. The market for renewable energy is set to grow, underpinned by proven technologies, robust financial instruments, and secure regulation. Europe is the current focus of this market and provides the best opportunities for infrastructure investors but in coming years will be joined by the United States and Asia.

ENDNOTES

1. United Nations Environment Program (UNEP). "Global Trends in Sustainable Energy Investment." 2009. http://sefi.unep.org/english/globaltrends2009.html. Accessed 11/27/2009.
2. World Alliance for Decentralized Electricity. www.localpower.org. Accessed 11/27/2009.
3. European Wind Energy Association Press Release. See www.ewea.org/index.php?id=60&no_cache=1&tx_ttnews[tt_news]=575&tx_ttnews[backPid]=1&cHash=d58584a791. Accessed 11/27/2009.
4. Danish Energy Agency, Energy Statistics, 2007. http://193.88.185.141/Graphics/UK_Facts_Figures/Statistics/yearly_statistics/2007/energy%20statistics%202007%20uk.pdf. Accessed 11/27/2009.
5. This is a simplification. The NPV of a project using WACC as a discount rate yields a positive value. Financial analysis of a power plant is much more complicated than the simple example given in the text.
6. Currently PV plants tend to be in excess of 5 MW. This example is for illustrative purposes only.
7. *Applying Portfolio Theory to EU Electricity Planning and Policy-making.* Shimon Awerbuch, 2003. www.awerbuch.com/shimonpages/shimondocs/iea-portfolio.pdf. Accessed 11/27/2009.
8. United Nations Environment Program (UNEP). "Global Trends in Sustainable Energy Investment." 2009. http://sefi.unep.org/english/globaltrends2009.html. Accessed 11/27/2009.

CHAPTER 8

Infrastructure and Union Labor

A Match Made in Heaven?

Michael D. Underhill
Founder, Capital Innovations LLC

The challenges of a successful infrastructure program, as it relates to labor unions, lies in the role of the fiduciary in protecting the interests of labor unions. The idea of double or triple bottom-line investing is nothing new and the investment strategies have taken the form of many real estate, property, and real asset investment strategies. The key to successful infrastructure investment programs for the labor unions is to chart a course for specific objectives that will be accomplished with each union's investment program. There needs to be a framework of primary, secondary, and tertiary objectives that are the focus for each union segment collectively. The credo of One Vision, One Voice, One Union works well in organizing membership, but it becomes more problematic when applied to investment strategies across labor union multi-employer retirement plans. What is "good" for the United Food and Commercial Workers Union (UFCW), may not be suitable investment objectives for Service Employees International Union (SEIU) or the International Brotherhood of Electrical Workers (IBEW). The optimal model portfolio of infrastructure investments may look very different for the unions mentioned here and other labor unions predicated upon their primary and collateral investment objectives.

Experienced investors continue to utilize diversification as a successful method to mitigate risk in investment programs, but risk becomes even more complex when layering on sustainability principles when constructing labor union infrastructure investment programs. A simple example of risk reduction as it applies to Greenfield infrastructure investing would be the application of Engineering, Procurement and Construction (EPC) contracts or insurance within the concession agreements. But imagine if one were to try to enforce responsible contractor policies (RCP) when a consortium of large investment banks were forcing your hand in a high-pressure bidding situation. It is not that simple. The need for enforcement of RCPs across the board with all projects when there is labor union investment dollars at work is imperative for successful sustainable infrastructure investing. This is accomplished through a relationship-driven approach to monitoring each and every project.

"Conventional wisdom" maintains that utilization of nonunion employees during infrastructure project construction saves time and money. Unfortunately more often the press and academics focus on union labor and infrastructure projects highlighting Project Labor Agreements (PLA) inefficiencies that incorporate "poor public policy that attempt to harm taxpayers, contractors and their employees."[1] Dr. John R. McGowan from St. Louis University authored a paper in October 2009 titled, "The Discriminatory Impact of Union Fringe Benefit Requirements on Nonunion Workers Under Government-Mandated Project Labor Agreements." The study found that in total, the move to Project Labor Agreements could cost nonunion workers and their employers from over $275 million to over $1.38 billion annually.

With studies such as this and a preponderance of evidence in the universe challenging the use of union labor in infrastructure projects, then how are union labor retirement programs, annuity benefits funds and other union-related investment funds to approach investing in infrastructure while adhering to collateral investment objectives that are pro-union labor? One of the techniques that has been utilized involves investing in infrastructure portfolio companies or publicly listed infrastructure equity securities that can provide for union labor employment objectives (job preservation and creation) while maintaining a high performing investment thesis long term or what we refer to as Sustainable Infrastructure Investing™.

TUTOR PERINI CORPORATION SUSTAINABLE INFRASTRUCTURE INVESTING CASE STUDY

Tutor Perini Corporation is a leading civil and building construction company offering diversified general contracting and design/build services to private clients and public agencies throughout the world. They have provided construction services since 1894 and have established a strong reputation in the infrastructure market by executing large complex projects on time and within budget while adhering to strict quality control measures.

The company offers general contracting, pre-construction planning and comprehensive project management services, including the planning and scheduling of the manpower, equipment, materials, and subcontractors required for a project. They also offer self-performed construction services including excavation, concrete forming and placement, steel erection, electrical and mechanical services, plumbing and HVAC. They are known for their major complex building project commitments as well as their capacity to perform large and complex transportation and heavy civil construction for government agencies and private clients throughout the world. The company operates with roughly 3,000 salaried staff and 25,000 skilled craftsmen that work on Tutor Perini infrastructure projects.[2]

Tutor Perini, in October 2009, decided to relocate their headquarters from Boston to Los Angeles, and labor union officials came from far and wide to show their appreciation at the celebration. Tutor Perini asserts that union labor is more efficient than their nonunion brethren when it comes to infrastructure projects and the quality of work is considerably better. "The Union craftsman training programs, education and on-the-job experience is reflected in project cost savings when these projects 'hit the mark' or come in ahead of schedule," stated Kenneth R. Burk, executive vice president and chief financial officer for Tutor Perini.

One recent example of union-labor efficiency is the newly completed $234 million Los Angeles Police headquarters building that came in ahead of schedule and under budget. Tutor Perini attributed this accomplishment to their use of skilled union labor and removing the inefficiencies associated with non-union contractors that often create delays and cost overruns.

Other infrastructure projects built by Tutor Perini include UCLA Westwood Hospital ($542 million), Los Angeles International Airport runway expansion ($242 million), San Francisco International Airport reconstruction program ($1.1 billion), Alameda Corridor ($783 million), BART subway extension ($710 million) and the Richmond/San Rafael Bridge retrofit ($762 million) and McCarran International Airport Terminal 3 ($1.2 billion).[3]

This is one of numerous case studies that can be applied to Sustainable Infrastructure Investing™ in a pro-union manner. Labor unions have a unique opportunity to utilize globally accepted principles in the realm of infrastructure investing that may change the way they put their pension fund money to work through more strategic investment. Application of The Principles for Responsible Investment and guidelines for incorporating environmental, social, and governance issues into infrastructure investment decision making and ownership practices will afford some unique insight into doing well and doing good for these unique investors.

UNITED NATIONS' PRINCIPLES FOR RESPONSIBLE INVESTMENT STATEMENT

Since their launch in 2006, support for the Principles has expanded and now includes over 375 signatories representing more than $13 trillion. The Principles are a framework for investors to help them consider environmental, social, and governance (ESG) issues in their investment decision-making processes. Supporters of the Principles believe that applying them will improve long-term financial returns while simultaneously aligning the goals of institutional investors with those of society at large.

Becoming a signatory is voluntary, yet demonstrates a clear commitment to the Principles and their implementation. Each year, signatories are invited to complete a survey discussing how they are putting the Principles into practice. The following six Principles listed below are guidelines for investors seeking to implement a program. Following, the principles illustrate practical application.

Principle 1: We will incorporate ESG issues into investment analysis and decision-making processes.

Union-labor pension and investment funds' ("institutional investor") investment policy describes how it integrates ESG issues into its investment decision making and ownership practices. Institutional investor strives to invest all of its assets in a socially responsible manner. When institutional investor meets with external investment managers, it regularly inquires how they are integrating ESG analyses into their investment strategies.

Principle 2: We will be active owners and incorporate ESG issues into our ownership policies and practices.

Institutional investor demonstrates its active ownership of investments through voting the proxy ballot of each company it owns. Institutional investor's proxy voting guidelines provide clear indications of how it votes on various ESG issues that are frequently addressed at corporate annual meetings. A record of the institutional investor's votes is available through its compliance department.

Institutional investor communicates directly with many of the companies it owns by writing letters, meeting with senior management, and filing shareholder proposals. Issues that may be addressed with companies include corporate sustainability, climate change, human rights, supply chains, HIV/AIDS, and governance.

As a result of its activities, institutional investor has witnessed changes in company policies, improved corporate disclosure, the establishment of new programs and initiatives, and a greater willingness by companies to work with investors and other stakeholders.

Principle 3: We will seek appropriate disclosure on ESG issues by the entities in which we invest.

In its communications with companies, institutional investor regularly encourages the disclosure of relevant ESG information, believing that increased transparency facilitates responsible corporate behavior and improves the investment decision-making process. Since adoption, institutional investor recommends companies review various frameworks and international standards as references to guide their actions and disclosures. These include the Global Reporting Initiative, the International Labour Code, the United Nations Global Compact, and the Universal Declaration of Human Rights.

Principle 4: We will promote acceptance and implementation of the Principles within the investment industry.

Institutional investor routinely discusses ESG issues with its investment managers and at conferences attended by other investors. In its relationships with managers, peer organizations, and others, institutional investor encourages the adoption and implementation of the Principles.

Principle 5: We will work together to enhance our effectiveness in implementing the Principles.

Institutional investor works collaboratively with a number of organizations and through a number of venues to promote a better understanding of ESG issues, to encourage the development of new research and tools and to coordinate activities. Institutional investor participates in the Interfaith Center on Corporate Responsibility (CERES) the Investor Network on Climate Risk, the Social Investment Forum, the International Working Group of the Social Investment Forum, and the Carbon Disclosure Project.

Principle 6: We will each report on our activities and progress toward implementing the Principles.

Four times a year, institutional investor publishes a newsletter that discusses how ESG issues are integrated into investment practices. Institutional investor's proxy voting record is publicly available, as is *a list of companies* that have failed to meet the agency's investment criteria and are barred from purchase. *A list of companies with which* institutional investor *has engaged*, including those at which shareholder proposals have been filed, is also available.

LABOR STANDARDS/HUMAN RIGHTS

Globalization has made us aware that, around the world, people work under vastly different circumstances. In some factories, particularly in developing countries, there are reports of forced overtime, low wages, unsafe working conditions, and child labor.

Institutional investors' first social creed was largely concerned with labor issues. Echoing concerns still keenly felt today, Institutional investors called "for a living wage in every industry," "the abolition of child labor," "for the principle of conciliation and arbitration in industrial dissensions" and, ultimately, "equal rights and complete justice for all men in all stations of life."

The social Principles assert that "every person has the right to a job at a living wage," "the right . . . to organize for collective bargaining" and the right "to refuse to work in situations that endanger health and/or life."

Accordingly, institutional investors adopting the Principles are an advocate for workers' rights. Of special concern are the working conditions in the overseas factories that supply U.S. companies with manufactured goods. Institutional investors should focus on companies that maintain and enforce clear codes of conduct for their various suppliers and global facilities. These codes are meant to guarantee that workers are treated humanely, compensated fairly, and allowed to organize without fear of intimidation or reprisal.

Corporate Governance

Traditionally, corporations have operated without much scrutiny from shareholders or the general public, but such corporation failures as Bear

Stearns and Lehman Brothers have increased the calls for greater corporate accountability and more open and transparent governance. Corporations should be responsible not only to their stockholders, but also to other stakeholders: their workers, suppliers, vendors, customers, the communities in which they do business, and for the earth, which supports them. Union labor funds that adopt ESG principles are supporting the public's right to know what impact corporations have in these various arenas.

Accordingly, institutional investors should be cognizant of how corporations are governed. In particular, focusing on numerous issues including:

- Boards of directors should reflect the diversity of society (more representation by women and minorities),
- Directors should be more accountable to shareholders through majority vote and annual elections, and
- The majority of directors, as well as the board chairperson, should be independent of company management (not employed by the company).

Taking the guidelines a step further and spelling out universal standards that can help public sector and labor union pension funds reach their investment and collateral goals is the next logical step toward sustainable infrastructure investing. There needs to be additional investment objectives and pro-labor objectives that can help bridge the "gap" (read chasm) between the two ideologies while permitting the other to accomplish their stated goals.

The balancing act of providing superior risk-adjusted investment returns while not sacrificing the ESG objectives requires the need to spell out in more detail investment policy as it relates to infrastructure and labor so that there is consensus before the investment are made. The environmental aspects of investment policy statements have been refined recently thanks in large part to groups like CERES (California Environmental Resources Evaluation System).

Environmentally Focused Policies
(Ms. Kirsten Spalding, CERES)

Environmental policy guidance for institutional investors has been available for public and labor sector pension funds and has recently been refined with the help of organizations like CERES (pronounced *series*), which is a national network of investors, environmental organizations, and other public interest groups working with companies and investors to address sustainability challenges such as global climate change.

CERES' mission is quite simple: Integrating sustainability into capital markets for the health of the planet and its people. CERES' Investor Network for Climate Risk focuses attention on the risks and opportunities from climate risk as they impact every asset class in an investor's portfolio. As investors are beginning to think about significant investments in infrastructure, they are incorporating a range of sustainability factors, and particularly climate risk into their due diligence around investment decision making and portfolio valuation.

At the 2008 Investor Summit for Climate Risk, investors in the CERES network adopted the following goal as part of their 2008 Action Plan: "Encourage debt and equity analysts, ratings agencies, and investment banks to incorporate climate risks, opportunities, and carbon costs into their analysis of a new category of investment funds—infrastructure—including transportation, water, and other projects needed to support the growth of cities and the transition to a low-carbon economy."[4]

Investors are acknowledging that not only are there unique risks to infrastructure investments, but that by their very nature, infrastructure investments have climate impacts that must be considered as these investments are made. Investment choices in infrastructure projects will have long-term impacts on the communities where these projects are developed. Investors can use a lens of smart growth principles with concern for the specific investment's energy efficiency, fuel economy, and alternative energy generation and distribution impacts as they consider investment opportunities.

Working closely with CERES, the California Public Employees Retirement System (CalPERS) adopted a strong investment policy for its new investments in infrastructure—the policy articulated the goal: Act as a responsible steward of program investments through quality services, responsible labor and management practices and responsible environmental practices.[5] CalPERS incorporated renewable energy and sustainability language into the policy and added a specific risk parameter that addressed climate risk.

This strong policy has led CalPERS to incorporate these concerns as priorities in their hiring of asset managers for this asset class. As CalPERS considers its first infrastructure investments, these issues are incorporated into their investment analysis.

CalPERS is one of the first state pension funds to develop a specific infrastructure investment policy. But many pension funds are now incorporating of sustainability issues into their general investment policies and their corporate governance policies. Investors are considering the climate and sustainability impacts of their public equity, clean tech private equity, real estate and their fixed income portfolios. As institutional investors seek to enhance the long term value and minimize risks to their holdings overall, CERES anticipates that they will incorporate this analysis into their due diligence on new infrastructure investment opportunities.

FIDUCIARY RESPONSIBILITIES, GOVERNANCE AND SUSTAINABLE INFRASTRUCTURE INVESTMENT

The need to layer in governance guidelines into infrastructure projects requires specific policy statements that incorporate numerous facets of the individual projects. As it relates to adhering to the requirements of our fiduciary obligations, investors should target investment in infrastructure projects and infrastructure funds that provide for attractive, long-term, risk-adjusted total returns, with an eye toward investment opportunities that provide cash flow from operations, an opportunity to participate in capital appreciation, inflation protection and diversification. These goals may be accomplished through the use of investment techniques that do not require excessive or inappropriate financial leverage.

Stimulate Job Creation

Brownfield (existing), Rehabilitative Brownfield, and Greenfield (new infrastructure projects) may be made with skilled, experienced labor that may cause greater efficiency and effectiveness in the course of project development. The ability to preserve jobs, protect wages and working conditions will be accomplished through the payment of prevailing wage.

Enhance Labor Solidarity

Utilizing project labor agreements that embody the standards of the building and construction trades and AFL-CIO to help maintain quality construction standards. These principles facilitate smooth work flow with projects by eliminating jobsite friction and work stoppages. Application of these standards will help trained and skilled workers to ensure timely completion of projects, advance well-engineered construction, manage costs, protect against strikes or lockouts, and provide resolution to jurisdictional disputes and grievances. In addition, these standards will sustain a pipeline of skilled and experienced labor that will incorporate strategic objectives such as inclusion employment strategies for minority and women contractors.

Neutrality

Investors should have target objectives stating that projects will promote labor neutrality for project employees not members of existing bargaining unit recognized under the National Labor Relations Act.

Employment Protection and Job Retention

When evaluating infrastructure projects that involve the sale, lease, or management of public assets, investors should be focused on the important role and contribution of public employees in the design, construction, and operation of such assets while reducing the probability of any adverse impact on public sector labor employment. Infrastructure projects should incorporate offers of employment under terms and conditions that provide comparable wages and benefits to the employees of the municipality at the time of the lease, with respect to the property used and provide for work that is performed by public employees and shall continue to be performed by public employees with a degree of consistency. Ongoing training and apprentice programs should be the focus for these projects as well to continue to grow and develop skilled labor for the future of our country.

These are merely a few points for consideration in building a sustainable infrastructure investment program; there are numerous challenges that lie ahead in the markets and public policy environment which both remain equally fluid for the foreseeable future. The good news for sustainable infrastructure investors is that steps have been taken by the Obama administration to help ease the burden toward labor and infrastructure growing together.

February 6, 2009 is a day that will go down in history as far as labor and infrastructure is concerned. On that day, President Obama signed an Executive Order authorizing federal executive agencies to use project labor agreements on federal construction contracts with a total cost of $25 million or more clearing the path for union labor job preservation and creation nationwide in the United States. Here is the order:[6]

Friday, February 6th, 2009 at 12:00 am

Executive Order: Use of Project Labor Agreements for Federal Construction Projects

THE WHITE HOUSE

Office of the Press Secretary

For Immediate Release

February 6, 2009

EXECUTIVE ORDER

- - - - - - -

USE OF PROJECT LABOR AGREEMENTS FOR FEDERAL CONSTRUCTION PROJECTS

By the authority vested in me as President by the Constitution and the laws of the United States of America, including the Federal Property and Administrative Services Act, 40 U.S.C. 101 *et seq.*, and in order to promote the efficient administration and completion of Federal construction projects, it is hereby ordered that:

Section 1. Policy. (a) Large-scale construction projects pose special challenges to efficient and timely procurement by the Federal Government. Construction employers typically do not have a permanent workforce, which makes it difficult for them to predict labor costs when bidding on contracts and to ensure a steady supply of labor on contracts being performed. Challenges also arise due to the fact that construction projects typically involve multiple employers at a single location. A labor dispute involving one employer can delay the entire project. A lack of coordination among various employers, or uncertainty about the terms and conditions of employment of various groups of workers, can create frictions and disputes in the absence of an agreed-upon resolution mechanism. These problems threaten the efficient and timely completion of construction projects undertaken by Federal contractors. On larger projects, which are generally more complex and of longer duration, these problems tend to be more pronounced.

(b) The use of a project labor agreement may prevent these problems from developing by providing structure and stability to large-scale construction projects, thereby promoting the efficient and expeditious completion of Federal construction contracts. Accordingly, it is the policy of the Federal Government to encourage executive agencies to consider requiring the use of project labor agreements in connection with large-scale construction projects in order to promote economy and efficiency in Federal procurement.

Sec. 2. Definitions. (a) The term "labor organization" as used in this order means a labor organization as defined in 29 U.S.C. 152(5).

(b) The term "construction" as used in this order means construction, rehabilitation, alteration, conversion, extension, repair, or improvement of buildings, highways, or other real property.

(c) The term "large-scale construction project" as used in this order means a construction project where the total cost to the Federal Government is $25 million or more.

(d) The term "executive agency" as used in this order has the same meaning as in 5 U.S.C. 105, but excludes the Government Accountability Office.

(e) The term "project labor agreement" as used in this order means a pre-hire collective bargaining agreement with one or more labor organizations that establishes the terms and conditions of employment for a specific construction project and is an agreement described in 29 U.S.C. 158(f).

Sec. 3. (a) In awarding any contract in connection with a large-scale construction project, or obligating funds pursuant to such a contract, executive agencies may, on a project-by-project basis, require the use of a project labor agreement by a contractor where use of such an agreement will (i) advance the Federal Government's interest in achieving economy and efficiency in Federal procurement, producing labor-management stability, and ensuring compliance with laws and regulations governing safety and health, equal employment opportunity, labor and employment standards, and other matters, and (ii) be consistent with law.

(b) If an executive agency determines under subsection (a) that the use of a project labor agreement will satisfy the criteria in clauses (i) and (ii) of that subsection, the agency may, if appropriate, require that every contractor or subcontractor on the project agree, for that project, to negotiate or become a party to a project labor agreement with one or more appropriate labor organizations.

Sec. 4. Any project labor agreement reached pursuant to this order shall:

(a) bind all contractors and subcontractors on the construction project through the inclusion of appropriate specifications in all relevant solicitation provisions and contract documents;

(b) allow all contractors and subcontractors to compete for contracts and subcontracts without regard to whether they are otherwise parties to collective bargaining agreements;

(c) contain guarantees against strikes, lockouts, and similar job disruptions;

(d) set forth effective, prompt, and mutually binding procedures for resolving labor disputes arising during the project labor agreement;

(e) provide other mechanisms for labor-management cooperation on matters of mutual interest and concern, including productivity, quality of work, safety, and health;

and

(f) fully conform to all statutes, regulations, and Executive Orders.

<u>Sec</u>. 5. This order does not require an executive agency to use a project labor agreement on any construction project, nor does it preclude the use of a project labor agreement in circumstances not covered by this order, including leasehold arrangements and projects receiving Federal financial assistance. This order also does not require contractors or subcontractors to enter into a project labor agreement with any particular labor organization.

<u>Sec</u>. 6. Within 120 days of the date of this order, the Federal Acquisition Regulatory Council (FAR Council), to the extent permitted by law, shall take whatever action is required to amend the Federal Acquisition Regulation to implement the provisions of this order.

<u>Sec</u>. 7. The Director of OMB, in consultation with the Secretary of Labor and with other officials as appropriate, shall provide the President within 180 days of this order, recommendations about whether broader use of project labor agreements, with respect to both construction projects undertaken under Federal contracts and construction projects receiving Federal financial assistance, would help to promote the economical, efficient, and timely completion of such projects.

<u>Sec</u>. 8. <u>Revocation of Prior Orders, Rules, and Regulations</u>. Executive Order 13202 of February 17, 2001, and Executive Order 13208 of April 6, 2001, are revoked. The heads of executive agencies shall, to the extent permitted by law, revoke expeditiously any orders, rules, or regulations implementing Executive Orders 13202 and 13208.

<u>Sec</u>. 9. <u>Severability</u>. If any provision of this order, or the application of such provision to any person or circumstance, is held to be invalid, the remainder of this order and the application of the provisions of such to any person or circumstance shall not be affected thereby.

<u>Sec</u>. 10. <u>General</u>. (a) Nothing in this order shall be construed to impair or otherwise affect:

(i) authority granted by law to an executive department, agency, or the head thereof; or

(ii) functions of the Director of the Office of Management and Budget relating to budgetary, administrative, or legislative proposals.

(b) This order shall be implemented consistent with applicable law and subject to the availability of appropriations.

(c) This order is not intended to, and does not, create any right or benefit, substantive or procedural, enforceable at law or in equity by any party against the United States, its departments, agencies, or entities, its officers, employees, or agents, or any other person.

Sec. 11. Effective Date. This order shall be effective immediately and shall apply to all solicitations for contracts issued on or after the effective date of the action taken by the FAR Council under section 6 of this order.

BARACK OBAMA

THE WHITE HOUSE,

February 6, 2009

ENDNOTES

1. Associated Builders and Contractors Union-Only PLA Studies. October 2009.
2. Tutor-Perini News Release, October 2009. http://investor.perini.com/phoenix. zhtml?c=106886&p=irol-newsArticle&ID=1344138&highlight=.
3. Ibid.
4. 2008 Investor Summit for Climate Risk, excerpt from 2008 Action Plan.
5. California Public Employees' Retirement System, Statement Of Investment Policy For The Inflation-Linked Asset Class, December 2008. www.calpers.ca.gov/eip-docs/investments/policies/inv-asset-classes/fixed-income/ILAC.pdf.
6. White House Briefing Room Press Release of Executive Order, February 6, 2009.

CHAPTER 9

How Valuation Can Vary Meaningfully

The Pennsylvania Turnpike

Daniel F. Huang
Director, Duff & Phelps, LLC

Dr. Stephan Forstmann
Managing Director, Duff & Phelps, LLC

VALUATION, IN ITS ESSENCE, IS A SIMPLE CONCEPT

Valuation, relatively speaking, is a simple concept—*What is something worth*? Determining the value of an investment, asset, or liability, however, is an entirely different matter. With complex infrastructure investments, value—like beauty—lies in the eye of the beholder.

As is typical in infrastructure projects, when there are a disparate multitude of concerned stakeholders—buyers, sellers, elected officials, government authorities, employees concerned for their jobs, the general public, local neighbors, key clients, financial intermediaries, end users—the issue of value becomes even more complex. Consider the proposed privatization of the Pennsylvania Turnpike.

In December 2006, Pennsylvania Governor Edward Rendell announced that the Commonwealth would solicit expressions of interest from private firms to determine the potential value of leasing or privatizing the 531-mile Pennsylvania Turnpike. "The turnpike is a valuable asset that was built by public employees and paid for by motorists. If in the future we decide that changing the way it is managed is valuable enough to Pennsylvania, we should definitely consider it. Nonetheless, the protection of the public will be our number one priority," said the Governor.[1] At the time, Governor Rendell indicated that preliminary estimates of what the Turnpike was worth varied widely, with values ranging anywhere from $2 billion up to $30 billion.[2]

In 2007, Morgan Stanley & Co. was selected as financial advisor to Governor Rendell's administration to provide an assessment of the amount that could be earned using various transaction structures. The ultimate decision of what to do with the turnpike would be the responsibility of Governor Rendell and the General Assembly.[3] Three options were evaluated:

1. A long-term lease of the turnpike;
2. Creation of a new, tax-exempt, public benefit corporation, which would allow for private management of the turnpike; and
3. A proposal by the Pennsylvania Turnpike Commission that included new tolls on Interstate 80 and a new "congestion tax" that would be collected at the most heavily used turnpike exits.

In May 2007, Governor Rendell announced that the analysis by Morgan Stanley indicated "a lease of the Pennsylvania Turnpike is likely to generate the highest level of funding to repair roads and bridges and avert drastic public transit cuts."[4] Morgan Stanley's analysis indicated that a long-term lease of the turnpike offered the highest potential, with upfront lease proceeds estimated to range from $12 billion to $18 billion. Morgan Stanley also noted that "It is difficult to accurately estimate revenue to the Commonwealth under a long-term lease; recent transactions have generated bids significantly higher than initial estimates," and that "estimates of market value were substantially exceeded in Chicago and Indiana," referring to the earlier lease transactions of the Chicago Skyway and Indiana Toll Road. Morgan Stanley also advised that, "the only way to resolve uncertainty over the value of a long-term lease is to enter the market and solicit bids" and that "enactment of authorizing legislation before a bid process begins is necessary to provide the best environment for maximizing revenue."[5]

Not surprisingly, value assessments of the turnpike by proponents, opponents, stakeholders, and others varied widely. The *Pittsburgh Post-Gazette* acknowledged that Morgan Stanley's $12 billion to $18 billion value was "admittedly an educated estimate."[6] A *BusinessWeek* cover story reported that "a lease of the Pennsylvania Turnpike could go for more than $30 billion."[7] In June 2007, the Pennsylvania Department of Transportation (PennDOT) received expressions of interest (but not formal bids) from 16 potential bidders regarding a potential 75-year Turnpike lease.[8]

In February 2008, the Democratic Caucus of the Pennsylvania House of Representatives released a study entitled "For Whom the Road Tolls" (FWTRT), which concluded the present value of a corporate lease would be $14.8 billion. However, according to that same study, a significantly greater present value could be realized under the existing Pennsylvania Turnpike Commission (PTC) Act 44 program, which would authorize PennDOT to lease the in-state portion of Interstate 80 to the PTC for conversion to a toll road and would require PTC to make a stream of payments for 50 years. Additionally, the same study determined that the PTC or a not-for-profit corporation would have a funding advantage over a corporate concessionaire and such a monetization would have a present value of $22.8 billion, a value again significantly higher than the long-term lease option as valued by the study.[9] Upon closer scrutiny, a Reason Foundation critique of FWTRT concluded that "FWTRT fails to make its case and is seriously flawed as a guide for Pennsylvania policymakers." The Reason Foundation, a nonpartisan public policy research group, also concluded that due to different assumptions used in two of the three valuations, it was "impossible for this to be an apples-to-apples comparison, since at least two key factors differ between the two cases."[10] The PTC, in response to the Reason Foundation's critique, concluded that the Reason Foundation's study of the Pennsylvania Turnpike's operating budget was "fundamentally flawed and reaches an erroneous conclusion that clearly reflects its author's political agenda."[11]

On May 9, 2008—17 months after Governor Rendell first solicited expressions of interest—PennDOT received formal bids from three bidding consortia. The low bid was reported to be $8.1 billion.[12] The top two bids received from groups led by Goldman Sachs and Abertis Infraestructuras/Citi Infrastructure Investors were within 10 percent of each other, and those two groups were given an additional week to prepare best-and-final offers. On May 16, a final bid of $12.1 billion was submitted by the group led by Goldman Sachs.[13] The Abertis/Citi consortium raised additional capital from lending institutions that had been supporting an earlier bidder and Albertis/Citi increased its earlier bid by more than $2 billion in the final round with a winning bid of $12.8 billion.[14]

"This is a great day for Pennsylvania," Governor Rendell said. "We urgently need new funding for road and bridge repair, and a turnpike lease will help us meet that need."[15]

At $12.8 billion, the Pennsylvania Turnpike would be the largest privatization of a U.S. infrastructure asset to date.[16] Reflecting on the deal, administration officials acknowledge that they expected a range of bids from $12 billion to $16 billion. But a number of legislators said they believed the bids would be as high as $30 billion.[17]

According to an analysis by The Pew Center on the States, "Governor Rendell asked the legislature to approve the Citi/Abertis $12.8 billion offer. The ensuing months of debate over the turnpike lease proposal were followed closely by the public and the press, and organizations favoring and opposing the concession produced reports to support their claims. Legislators were besieged with information and input from lobbyists, research organizations, media, and constituents. "There was fuzzy math; there was misinformation; and there was pure spin," says Representative Rick Geist, Republican co-chair of the House Transportation Committee and a proponent of the deal. "The misinformation was almost to the point that people thought the Spaniards were going to take the highway and move it back to Spain." Legislative debate became stuck around several factors, including the state's financial assumptions and the proposed oversight mechanism. . . . When the legislature failed to vote on the proposal by the end of September 2008, the [Abertis/Citi] consortium withdrew its bid."[18]

As previously mentioned, *valuation*—relatively speaking—is a simple concept. Determining the value of an investment, asset or liability, however, is an entirely different matter.

For the Pennsylvania Turnpike (or any other investment for that matter), valuation should be reflective of the structure of the transaction, the risk profile, and other factors. With the Pennsylvania Turnpike, a vast range of values for the potential realizable upfront proceeds were presented over the course of two years by disparate groups that often had tangential interests. The Concession and Lease Agreement was a 686-page document (single-spaced). Without having transparency on the inputs and assumptions that went into determining the values different stakeholders ascribed to the turnpike, it is difficult—perhaps impossible—to make informed comparisons among the various options presented. Key inputs such as future payments to the Commonwealth, relative risks and rewards, and reasonableness of both the performance assumptions used in various options as well as the assumptions applied to the projected investment returns the Commonwealth would earn on the proceeds received are all factors that need to be taken into consideration in such an exercise. Governor Rendell's administration augmented its decision-making process by engaging experienced financial advisors. Stakeholders and interested parties further removed from the process, including the media (and, in part, the public, other elected officials, and numerous other constituents) did not have the benefit of reviewing the myriad of nuances inherent in each valuation presented over the two-year period to form a fully informed opinion, but they had opinions nonetheless as was their right to have them.

WHOSE VALUE IS IT ANYWAY?

Valuations are performed for any number of different purposes—merger and acquisition, disposition, monitoring, financial reporting, and tax reporting to name a few. Depending on the purpose of the valuation, the calculated monetary value ascribed to an investment or asset may not always match up.

One must ask, who is relying on the valuation—the seller, buyer, employees, end-users, competitors? When there is a limited supply of assets (such as toll roads, ports, airports, and railways), what is it worth to a bidder to win an asset (whether it's leasing, managing, or owning the asset)? Looking at it a different way, what is it worth to a bidder to prevent its competitors from winning the asset? Abertis/Citi's winning bid for the Pennsylvania Turnpike was reportedly over $2 billion more than its initial bid submitted one week earlier. Over the course of those seven days, the Pennsylvania Turnpike did not change, but clearly the bidders' willingness to pay for the right to lease the toll road was fully tested via the auction process.

Fair Value

The Financial Accounting Standards Board (FASB) issued Accounting Standards Codification Topic 820 (ASC 820)—*Fair Value Measurements and Disclosures* (which was originally issued as Statement of Financial Accounting Standards [SFAS] No. 157) in 2006, which became effective in November 2007. ASC 820's intention was to introduce a consistent definition of fair value, establish a framework for measuring fair value, and expand disclosures about fair value measurements. While ASC 820 has had a significant impact on the manner in which valuations are calculated and reported by many practitioners, it is important to recognize that the concept of fair value is not a new one, and fair value has been referenced by FASB well before the issuance of ASC 820 in 2006.

ASC 820 (and its amendments) currently defines fair value as "the price that would be received to sell an asset or paid to transfer a liability in an orderly transaction (that is, not a forced liquidation or distressed sale) between market participants at the measurement date under current market conditions."[19] ASC 820 introduced the concept of an "exit price" as well as a hierarchy of inputs to use in fair value measurement. Entities that report their financial statements in accordance with U.S. generally accepted accounting principles (GAAP) are required to report fair value and, therefore, are required to report those assets and liabilities carried at fair value consistent with ASC 820.

While the recent market turmoil (beginning in 2007) and the subsequent analysis of potential causes of such turmoil have put into question the exit price concept, fair value is—and has for a long time been—broadly recognized as an appropriate and applicable principle for representing value. The International Accounting Standards Board (IASB) is considering an International Financial Reporting Standard (IFRS) *Fair Value Measurement* that proposes defining fair value as "the price that would be received to sell an asset or paid to transfer a liability in an orderly transaction between market participants at the measurement date."[20]

The definitions of fair value applied by the FASB and IASB as well as the Government Accounting Standards Board (GASB) may vary in their wording, but the principle of fair value (fundamentally, a transaction that is executed between a willing buyer and a willing seller) is consistent with that of ASC 820.[21]

Why Does Fair Value Matter? Fair value reporting standards were driven, in part, by demands for greater transparency and disclosure in financial reporting. Fair value measurement establishes a framework that allows an "apples to apples" comparison of investment opportunities through the application of consistent inputs, assumptions, and valuation methodologies. In the absence of robust fair value reporting, the comparisons and observations being made on an opportunity may be more akin to comparing apples to oranges to Sylvester Stallone movies.

Furthermore,

- Most investors are (or are likely to soon be) required by relevant applicable GAAP to report their investments on a fair value basis;
- The use of a single consistent valuation standard such as fair value allows managers to make interim investment decisions on a comparable basis;
- Fair value provides a comparable basis for monitoring interim performance in the context of exercising the investor's fiduciary duty; and
- An arbitrary reporting basis such as initial investment cost does not allow comparability.

Methods for Determining Fair Value

The three most commonly accepted valuation methodologies are the market approach, income approach, and cost approach. The selection of a valuation technique or a combination of valuation techniques for each asset will depend on the particular circumstances.

The income and market approaches are typically used most prevalently when estimating the value of a going-concern business (that is, a business that functions without the intention or threat of liquidation for the foreseeable future), while the cost approach typically comes into play for distressed assets or assets that either don't or won't produce predictable cash flows. While both tax and financial reporting standards typically mandate that all available approaches should be considered in determining the fair value of a subject asset or liability, the general preference for practitioners in regards to infrastructure assets (that are not publicly traded) is to rely on the income approach and support the analysis with observations from collaborating data using the market approach.

The Income Approach   This approach estimates the enterprise value of a business (being the value of the complete capital structure of a business, i.e., the value available to satisfy the return expectations of all stakeholders, including debt and equity holders) based on the cash flows that the business can be expected to generate in the future. The income approach requires a projection of revenues and expenses specifically attributable to the business. The discounted cash flow (DCF) method, the most widely used application of the income approach, is then applied to convert the projected after-tax cash flows to their present value equivalents using a rate of return commensurate with the risk of achieving the asset's projected cash flow stream. The present value of the estimated after-tax cash flows during the discrete projection period is then added to the present value of the residual or terminal value, if any, to derive an estimate of value, which, mathematically, represents the value of all cash-flow streams beyond the projection period. If interested in the value of the common equity capital in the business, the enterprise value is then reduced by the fair value of all capital tranches that have preference in a liquidation scenario to the (common) equity to derive at the equity value of the business (e.g., all debt and preferred equity is subtracted, commonly at par, from the enterprise value to arrive at equity value).

The Market Approach   This approach in its most common form estimates the enterprise value of a business based on values of minority interests in publicly traded guideline companies that are then adjusted for control premia and lack of marketability discounts, as applicable (market comparable company method). Another variation of the market approach indicates the value of a business based on prices paid in actual transactions and on asking prices for controlling interests in companies offered for sale (market comparable transaction method). The process essentially involves comparison and correlation of the subject business with other similar companies.

Adjustments for differences in size, growth, profitability, risk, and return on investment, among others, are also considered.

The income approach recognizes the uniqueness of the subject assets being valued. Its fundamental difference from the market approach is the ability to separately quantify many financial and operating assumptions and consolidate them into an evaluation of a particular subject asset. The reasonableness of the result using the income approach largely depends on the reasonableness of the underlying cash flow projections. These projections are a reflection of the political, economic, and business fundamentals in which the business enterprise operates as of the date of the valuation. However, because events and circumstances often do not occur as expected, there will usually be differences between prospective financial information and actual results, and those differences may be material.

The Cost Approach This approach may also be employed, which, in its most common form, considers the amount that currently would be required to replace the service capacity of an asset (often referred to as *current replacement cost*). The cost approach estimates the current amount required to acquire or construct a substitute asset of comparable utility, adjusted for obsolescence. Obsolescence encompasses physical deterioration, functional obsolescence, and economic obsolescence and is broader than the concept of depreciation for financial reporting purposes (which usually is an allocation of historical cost) or tax purposes (usually based on specified service lives).[22] Greenfield development projects are often valued using the cost approach, when the enterprise is not fully operational, and when historical performance information is not meaningfully available and where neither the income approach nor market approach may yield sensible results. Similarly, subject assets whose ability to act as a going-concern is considered questionable (i.e., distressed assets) are commonly valued using a version of the cost approach.

Solid Waste in, Solid Waste Out?

The inputs and assumptions relied upon in determining value will fall into one of two categories: observable data or unobservable data. Observable data are those that reflect the assumptions that market participants would use in pricing the asset (e.g., comparable transactions and multiples derived using market comparables). Unobservable data include the practitioner's own assumptions about market assumptions based on the best information available in the circumstances (such as the practitioner's expectations for future growth or cost savings).

In practice, when determining fair value it is important to understand the quality of the data on which the valuation relies. For example, while observable data may be obtainable (for example, a private transaction between a buyer and seller) it should be determined whether the transaction did in fact occur between a willing buyer and willing seller in an orderly transaction. Did extraneous considerations or pressures exist that forced either the seller or the buyer of the comparable transaction to complete the transaction? Such information is often incomplete (or missing entirely) to the outside observer (that is, *you*, the person performing the valuation). There may be situations when a practitioner possesses weak observable data compared to more reliable unobservable data, and thoughtful judgment is critical in the application of fair value determination.[23]

Multiple Approaches

Valuation, it should be noted, is not an exact science. While the fair value of actively traded securities provides reliable indicators of the value of an enterprise (where share price multiplied by total number of shares = total value), the valuation of illiquid and hard-to-value assets requires much deeper analysis and substantial judgment, by definition making it subjective. Practitioners should be biased toward methodologies that draw heavily on market-based measures of risk and return. Generally speaking, fair value estimates based entirely on observable market data (if that market can be considered to be a fair reflection of value, i.e., if there is sufficient activity in said market) can be expected to be of greater reliability (and are certainly easier to defend or support) than those based on subjective assumptions, but for complex infrastructure assets, observable market data may often be unattainable, limited, or not fully applicable to the asset or opportunity being valued.

A robustly determined valuation should consider multiple valuation methodologies to ensure both observable and unobservable data and assumptions are being weighed appropriately. For opportunities when a bidder may own or operate an asset for 10 years, 30 years or even longer, the income approach is considered to be the more applicable valuation approach as it best allows the growth potential and changing cash flow profiles (over the course of the investment period) to be reflected. However, a robust valuation should also take into account the results derived from the market approach (and cost approach as applicable) to corroborate that the concluded value derived from the income approach is reasonable.

Sectors where there are a large universe of companies (both public and privately held) which are, either in their entirety or on a piece-meal basis (i.e., share by share), bought, sold, and financed on a fairly regular basis would, generally speaking, rely more heavily on observable indicators of value, such as the pricing of recent comparable transactions, earnings multiples of comparable companies, as well as industry benchmarks. Broadly speaking, reliable market data is often available for the following sectors:

- Regulated utilities—electricity distribution, transmission, gas, water
- Contracted—communications, oil and gas, district energy, power generation, waste, renewable energy
- Social infrastructure—hospitals, aged care, schools and universities, prisons
- Infrastructure-related: parking garages, telecom systems

For sectors where there are relatively fewer opportunities or comparable subject assets available (such as toll roads, airports, railways, and container ports), the quality and reasonableness of the inputs and assumptions are critically important in arriving at a robust and supportable valuation of an opportunity. In particular, although certain market data exists, DCF valuations are particularly applicable for the following assets:

- Throughput—airports, roads, tunnels, bridges, container terminals, rail

THANK YOU FOR VALUING THE FRIENDLY SKIES

The accuracy of the inputs and reasonableness of the assumptions applied will support a robust valuation, clearly. A granular analysis of the drivers and risks, and revenues and expenses, is necessary to arrive at a supportable and robust valuation, and the reasonableness of the assumptions and inputs used is critical.

The following outline provides an illustration of the level of complexity inherent in a robust valuation analysis, and lists typical procedures taken and inputs considered in valuing, by way of example, an airport lease concession agreement. A robust valuation process would involve gathering of pertinent information, consideration of performance metrics and risks factors, and evaluation of income and expense items and assumptions.

Typical valuation procedures would include:

- Obtaining an understanding of the lease concession agreement within the framework of the airport management industry.

- Analyzing general market data, including economic, governmental and environmental factors, that may affect the value of the concession.
- Reviewing the history, current state, and future possibilities of the airport subject to the concession contract.
- Analyzing the airport's historical financial and operating information.
- Analyzing the overall airport's and the concession's financial and operating projections and prospective information (including fee revenues, administrative expenses, net operating margins, working capital investments, and capital expenditures), including an analysis of historical operating and financial results, industry results and expectations, and management representations.
- Evaluating the most appropriate valuation model (e.g., income approach—single period model; income approach—multiperiod model; or market approach) and discount rates to be employed for each contract.
- Analyzing other facts and data considered pertinent to the valuation to arrive at a conclusion of value for the concession contract.

Key performance metrics to consider would include:

- Passenger airline aeronautical revenue
- Enplanements
- Passenger airline cost per enplanement
- Landed weights
- Signatory landing fee rates
- Annual aircraft operations
- Operating costs per passenger
- Earnings before interest, taxes, depreciation, and amortization (EBITDA) per passenger
- EBITDA margin

Typical investment risks to be considered in the determination of the appropriate discount rate for an airport would include:

- Investment risk
- Customer risk—airline quality, diversification of airline companies
- Regulatory and reporting risks
- Financial risks—liquidity, interest rates, currency, debt profile
- Legal risks—contract enforceability, covenants, litigation
- Operational—costs per enplanement, geographic spread, employees, processes, infrastructure, technology, systems, outsourcing

- Environmental and social risks
- Project risks
- Asset performance risks
- Occupational, health, and safety risks
- Reputation risks
- Strategic risks

As would be expected, numerous sources of revenue may be considered, from both passenger and nonpassenger sources as well as operating and nonoperating sources:

- Passenger airline aeronautical revenue
  - Passenger airline landing fees
  - Terminal arrival fees, rents, and utilities
  - Terminal area apron charges/tiedowns
  - Federal inspection fees
  - Other
- Nonpassenger aeronautical revenue
  - Landing fees from cargo
  - Landing fees from general aviation and military
  - Fixed base operations revenue
  - Cargo and hangar rentals
  - Aviation fuel tax retained for airport use
  - Fuel sales net profit/loss
  - Security reimbursement from federal government
  - Other
- Nonaeronautical revenue
  - Land and nonterminal facility leases and revenues
  - Terminal—food and beverage
  - Terminal—retail stores and duty free
  - Terminal—services and other
  - Rental cars
  - Parking and ground transportation
  - Hotel
  - Other
- Nonoperating revenue and capital contributions
  - Interest income
  - Grant receipts
  - Passenger facility charges
  - Capital contributions
  - Other

Expense line items for an airport would include both operating and nonoperating expenses:

- Operating expenses
  - Personnel compensation and benefits
  - Communications and utilities
  - Repairs and maintenance
  - Marketing/advertising/promotions
  - Supplies and materials
  - Contractual services
  - Insurance, claims, and settlements
  - Depreciation
  - Other
- Nonoperating expenses
  - Interest expense
  - Special items (extraordinary losses)
  - Other

Ongoing Financial Reporting: Mark-to-Market or Mark-to-Model?

After the airport concession agreement is won, the new operator would very likely be required to report the fair value of the concession agreement on a recurring basis (for investor reporting, audit purposes, and other reporting needs). For all the same reasons that a mark-to-market valuation was likely not possible when first valuing the concession agreement, ongoing valuations would require updating the inputs and assumptions that originally went into the DCF valuation model to reflect known or knowable data as of the new measurement date. In addition to having updated operating and financial performance of the asset (i.e., allowing for a comparison of actual performance versus the original investment plan), changes in market considerations such as applicable interest rates, discount rates, and future expectations for the sector should be taken into consideration. As noted previously, ASC 820 introduces the concept of an exit price, and even if the owner has the intention of owning or operating an asset for years to come, fair value reporting under U.S. GAAP would require that the value of the concession agreement reflect the price that would be received from a willing buyer to a willing seller as of the measurement date.

The market approach would provide further guidance to support the valuation derived by the income approach. The market approach will provide directional insight into the prices or multiples at which willing buyers and willing sellers are conducting comparable transactions, and will also show where valuations for publicly traded comparable companies have moved since the original transaction investment date.

It is generally important that recurring valuations after the original investment date be performed in a consistent manner. Any deviations from the original investment methodology in terms of key assumptions or projections should be documented for future reference.

BEST PRACTICES

In light of fair value reporting trends, it would be useful (if not imperative) that reported fair values for illiquid and hard-to-value assets are not only accurate, but are also supported by a well-defined and consistently applied valuation process that complies with the relevant reporting standards internationally.

Given the latitude and judgment involved in determining fair value, investors quite commonly augment their internal valuation processes with an independent, third-party review of the fair value policies, procedures, and conclusions of value. By involving advisors who are completely independent of sales, trading, and other commercial functions within the investor's organization, additional transparency is achieved and the investor is further able to demonstrate to its board, auditor, and other stakeholders that its valuation assessments are appropriate.

Accurate estimates of fair value resulting from sound valuation policy, well documented and consistently applied, is a requirement for investors in alternative assets, including infrastructure.

Valuation best practices would include:

- Establishing a formal, well-documented, and comprehensive valuation policy.
- Developing practical valuation procedures and methodologies consistent with the written policy and adhered to by deal teams and other valuation professionals on a daily basis.
- Establishment of an internal valuation committee to review and confirm the valuation conclusions.
- Preparing a well-documented investment memoranda for each investment at the time of investment with appropriate supporting details, including both qualitative and quantitative information and updating this memorandum at each measurement date (i.e., each time the value is to be reported to stakeholders).

- Incorporating an independent review of valuation policies, procedures and valuation conclusions by third-party valuation experts.
- Applying all applicable generally accepted valuation methodologies when valuing an investment, employed separately based on their relative merits, and then reaching a valuation conclusion after weighing each individual valuation result appropriately.
- Incorporating thoughtful and supportable inputs and assumptions used in valuations.
- Performing additional due diligence on companies and industries to assess appropriateness of fair values.
- Incorporating a yield analysis (which is a type of income approach) to determine the impact a change in market yields and company-specific risk (i.e., company rating) would have on the appropriate discount rate for liability cash flows.
- Requiring independent third-party appraisals on at least certain investments on a recurring basis (annually).
- Reviewing annually the written valuation policy to ensure continued compliance with stated procedures.

Benefits of the application of a best practices policy include:

- The investor gains an enhanced ability to demonstrate and support compliance with financial reporting requirements.
- All stakeholders—including regulators, boards, investors, independent auditors, and employees—gain increased confidence in the financial reporting and, as a result, management as a whole.
- The investor is able to provide evidence of critical core competencies.
- The investor (and its constituents) will benefit from enhanced risk management resulting from additional structure and discipline around the regular monitoring of investments.

CONCLUSION

Valuation is not an exact science. Valuation in its ultimate application tends to be very complex and requires substantial judgment when determining fair value. When stakeholders who are not familiar with nor very accustomed to the intricacies involved in determining a robust valuation are required to have an opinion on value (or worse, decide on value), the process and final outcome can be (to put it politely) bumpy.

With the Pennsylvania Turnpike example (which it should be noted is not unique to either Pennsylvania or to turnpikes), it should not be a surprise that hugely disparate valuation assessments were arrived at, depending on whom you ask (and depending on what their perspectives and intentions might have been). Nevertheless, valuations of complex infrastructure assets can be robustly determined by employing a methodical and consistent valuation approach that utilizes reasonable inputs and assumptions. Results based on such a robust process, if appropriately documented, will be defendable, explainable, and as such, important for all stakeholders in encouraging thoughtful debate and ultimately helping constituents in making better-informed decisions. And at the end of the day, the first step in bringing disparate (and often opposing) groups together for a common good is by creating constructive dialogue founded on accurate and balanced information. In the realm of infrastructure, inserting robustly determined fair valuations into the dialogue is a critical element that will benefit all stakeholders.

ENDNOTES

1. Commonwealth of Pennsylvania, "Governor Rendell Gauges Private Financial Interest in PA Turnpike; Analysis of Offers Could Help Determine Potential Value," Commonwealth of Pennsylvania, www.state.pa.us/papower/cwp/view.asp?A=11&Q=458517.
2. Barnes, Tom, "Want to Buy a Turnpike? Better Hurry Up," *Pittsburgh Post-Gazette*, December 7, 2006, www.postgazette.com/pg/06341/744229-147.stm.
3. Commonwealth of Pennsylvania, "Governor Rendell Announces Selection of Financial Advisor for Transportation Funding Options," Commonwealth of Pennsylvania, www.state.pa.us/papower/cwp/view.asp?A=11&Q=461198.
4. Commonwealth of Pennsylvania, "Governor Rendell Says Transportation Funding Analysis Determines Highest Value Likely from Long-Term Lease," Commonwealth of Pennsylvania, www.state.pa.us/papower/cwp/view.asp?A=11&Q=463354.
5. Morgan Stanley, "Transportation Funding Alternatives Involving the Pennsylvania Turnpike. Summary of Preliminary Findings," May 21, 2007.
6. Barnes, Tom, "Turnpike Lease Looks Good on Paper. Rendell Advisers Present a Study Seeing Potential for Big Profits," *Pittsburgh Post-Gazette*, May 22, 2007, www.post-gazette.com/pg/07142/788007-147.stm.
7. Thornton, Emily, "Roads to Riches. Why Investors are Clamoring to Take Over America's Highways, Bridges, and Airports—and Why the Public Should be Nervous." *BusinessWeek*, May 7, 2007, www.businessweek.com/magazine/content/07_19/b4033001.htm.
8. Commonwealth of Pennsylvania, "In Spirit of Compromise, Governor Rendell Shares Confidential Turnpike Info with General Assembly to Move

Funding Solution Forward," Commonwealth of Pennsylvania, June 12, 2007, www.state.pa.us/papower/cwp/view.asp?A=11&Q=464110.

9. Gray, Gary J., Cusatis, Patrick J., and Foote, John H., "For Whom the Road Tolls: Corporate Asset or Public Good. An Analysis of Financial and Strategic Alternatives for the Pennsylvania Turnpike," Democratic Caucus of the Pennsylvania House of Representatives, February 2008, www.pahouse.com/docs/For %20Whom%20the%20Road%20Tolls%20Final%202-23-081_FINAL.pdf.

10. Poole, Robert W., Jr, and Samuel, Peter, "Pennsylvania Turnpike Alternatives: A Review and Critique of the Democratic Caucus Study," Reason Foundation Policy Brief No. 70, April 2008, www.reason.org/pb70.pdf.

11. Pennsylvania Turnpike Commission, "PA Turnpike Calls Group's 'Study' Fatally Flawed," Pennsylvania Turnpike Commission, April 11, 2008, www .paturnpike.com/I80/news/nr041108.aspx.

12. Barnett, Megan, "America's Priciest Highway. Will Pennsylvania's Turnpike Land in Citi's Hands? Should It?" Conde Naste Portfolio.com, May 19, 2008, www.portfolio.com/news-markets/top-5/2008/05/19/Pennsylvania-Turnpike-Privatization.

13. Commonwealth of Pennsylvania, "Pennsylvania Turnpike Lease Would Boost Funding for Roads, Bridges, Transit. $12.8 Billion Payment Would Produce More Funding at Lower Cost to Drivers; Cancel Need for I-80 Tolls," Commonwealth of Pennsylvania, May 19, 2008, www.portal.state.pa.us/portal/ server.pt?open=512&objID=2999&PageID=431162&mode=2&contentid= http://pubcontent.state.pa.us/publishedcontent/publish/global/news_releases/ governor_s_office/news_releases/pennsylvania_turnpike_lease_would_boost_ funding_for_roads_bridges_transit.html.

14. The Pew Center on the States, "Driven By Dollars. What States Should Know When Considering Public-Private Partnerships to Fund Transportation," March 2009, www.pewtrusts.org/uploadedFiles/wwwpewtrustsorg/Reports/ State_policy/PA_Turnpike_FINAL_WEB.pdf.

15. Commonwealth of Pennsylvania, "Pennsylvania Turnpike Lease Would Boost Funding for Roads, Bridges, Transit."

16. Sorkin, Andrew Ross, "The Great Government Sell-Off," *New York Times*, DealBook, May 21, 2008,. http://dealbook.blogs.nytimes.com/2008/05/21/the-great-government-sell-off/.

17. The Pew Center on the States, "Driven By Dollars."

18. Ibid.

19. Financial Accounting Standards Board, Accounting Standards Codification §820 (formerly Statement of Financial Accounting Standards 157, *Fair Value Measurements*).

20. International Accounting Standards Board, Exposure Draft—Fair Value Measurement ED/2009/5, May, 2009.

21. Similarly the current (U.S.) tax definition of *fair market value* is based on the well-established and time-tested concept of "willing buyer and willing seller, neither under any compulsion to buy or sell" initially based on IRS Revenue Ruling 1959-60.

22. AICPA, "New Accounting Rules for Valuing and Reporting Investments in Plan Financial Statements," December 2008, http://ebpaqc.aicpa.org/NR/rdonlyres/ 104F1694-671E-4107-AC76-F50A17AE2B42/0/Summary_of_FAS_157.pdf.

23. ASC 820 requires the qualification of the type of input used (into Level I, II, or III) and to disclose which input level was used to value the subject assets. The use of the word *level* is misleading in that Level I inputs (i.e., market prices), for example, are not to be considered more reliable than Level II or III inputs.

CHAPTER 10

What Is Listed Infrastructure?

Michael D. Underhill
Founder, Capital Innovations LLC

*T*he *Compact Oxford English Dictionary* defines *infrastructure* as "the basic physical and organizational structures (e.g., buildings, roads, and power supplies) needed for the operation of a society or enterprise." *Infrastructure assets*, simply defined, represent a broad mix of the large-scale public systems, services, and facilities of a country or region that are necessary for economic activity to function. Some examples of infrastructure include power generation and transmission, water supplies and wastewater treatment, public transportation, rail, roads, bridges, tunnels, ports, airports, telecommunications, and finally, basic social services such as schools and hospitals.

The global listed infrastructure market represents a market value of roughly $1.79 trillion of outstanding securities currently in the market.[1] In a July 2008 market commentary report by Invesco Private Capital, global infrastructure needs are projected to be about $50 trillion in Organization for Economic Co-operation and Development(OECD) countries between 2005 and 2030.

WHAT IS INFRASTRUCTURE?

Infrastructure has emerged as its own differentiated asset class providing unique investment characteristics. Part of what defines infrastructure assets is that they provide a necessary good or service to society and they have a monopolistic position in their market with high barriers to entry for competitors. Given these characteristics, infrastructure assets tend to be highly regulated, which result in investments with distinct qualities.

Infrastructure assets usually are built to have long useful lives given that they provide a vital service and are expensive to construct. Additionally, the demand for the output from these assets tends to be inelastic given the scarcity of the resource being offered. With the pricing power that results from their position in the market, the revenue growth from these assets is typically limited to the rate of inflation by regulators. These factors result in infrastructure investments being able to offer long-term stable cash flows that have the potential for inflation hedging. In addition, infrastructure assets tend to have high barriers to entry, providing monopoly-like features.

Another characteristic of infrastructure investments is that they exhibit a hybrid nature of both fixed income cash flows coupled with capital gains. They behave somewhat like a bond with their stable cash flows and provide investors the ability to participate in capital appreciation or equity upside potential as the underlying assets appreciate in value. These assets can be improved upon and their capacity can be expanded allowing for their principal value to grow over time. The best opportunity for capital gains comes from investments involving development risk or monopoly businesses.

Finally, infrastructure investments do offer a variety of risk and return profiles. Infrastructure investments range from low-risk regulated assets to moderate-risk loosely regulated entities such as energy production. The assets offer varying amounts of inflation protection and different levels of vulnerability to economic cycles. These long-duration investments tend to be linked to inflation and they also offer low correlations with relative returns of other assets. It is important to note that while these assets are all considered the same asset class, not all of them will exhibit the same risk and return behavior.

WHAT IS THE INFRASTRUCTURE OPPORTUNITY?

Global demographic trends are driving the need for infrastructure construction in the world's developing economies. Brazil, China, and India have shifted from agrarian to industrial, urban societies. Including Russia in the mix, the BRIC (Brazil, Russia, India, and China) countries account for 40 percent of the world's population and an ever-increasing amount of the world's gross domestic product (GDP). These countries require new, modern infrastructure in order to facilitate the expansion of industry, the urbanization of their economies, and the effects of continued population growth and an expanding middle class.

In the developed markets, the infrastructure is mature and in a state of disrepair, having been constructed in the middle of the twentieth century. The percent of GDP that is spent on infrastructure has been steadily declining

EXHIBIT 10.1 American Society of Civil Engineers 2009 Report Card for America's Infrastructure

Aviation	D
Bridges	C
Dams	D
Drinking water	D−
Energy	D+
Hazardous waste	D
Inland waterways	D−
Levees	D−
Public parks and recreation	C−
Rail	C−
Roads	D−
Schools	D
Solid waste	C+
Transit	D
Wastewater	D−

Source: American Society of Civil Engineers 2009 Report Card for America's Infrastructure.

for decades in most developed economies, leaving them with a crumbling legacy. This entire supply of old infrastructure needs to be either repaired or replaced.

The amount of investment that is required to fix or upgrade existing infrastructure in the developed economies is truly stunning, especially when one examines the state of the union in the United States. The American Society of Civil Engineers has estimated that the infrastructure funding needs are $2.2 trillion over a five-year period in the United States.

The United States' infrastructure currently holds a D average (see Exhibit 10.1).[2]

Even more disconcerting, funding levels as a share of all federal expenditures have remained at the same level as they were more than 20 years ago. The United States' crumbling infrastructure has been well documented over the past few years. The ready supply of capital for projects is eclipsed by the demand for infrastructure, which is driven by:

- Population growth
- Urbanization
- Aging infrastructure
- Favorable economic/political climate

Over the years, the U.S. government has driven the responsibility for the growth and upkeep of the United States' infrastructure down to the state and municipal levels. The states have found that they have been unable to meet the capital requirements of this task. More recently, the economic downturn has reduced all of the familiar sources of revenue for the states. Real estate taxes, income taxes, and sales taxes have all declined precisely when the need for capital is the greatest. With the states' inability to overcome a budget deficit from year to year, they have been unable to generate the capital for essential improvements to their infrastructure. The states are at a crossroads and many are now beginning to court private investors in order to fill their budget gaps.

Recently, the commitment to building the United States' future through stimulus efforts in infrastructure spending and project development has provided the much needed lift to job creation. In addition to the long-term trends that are benefitting this asset class, the stimulus package recently enacted by the U.S. government will benefit this sector directly in the near term.

The American Recovery and Reinvestment Act of 2009 (ARRA) was an economic stimulus package enacted by the U.S. Congress and signed into law by President Obama in February 2009. ARRA was largely based on Obama's proposals and was intended to provide economic stimulus in the wake of the financial crisis of 2008. The measures contained in the Act were worth $787 billion. The Act included federal tax relief, expansion of benefits, and domestic spending on education, health care, and infrastructure. The infrastructure investment in the Act totaled nearly $81 billion with core investments in roads and bridges, railways, sewers, and other transportation projects totaling over $51 billion.

Investors are viewing listed infrastructure as another "club" in their golf bag, offering them alternative access to a dynamic market opportunity. The liquidity and transparency have become more attractive than ever in today's opaque investment environment. The ability to generate income and total return explains some of its recent gain in popularity, particularly after the thrashing of most investment portfolios in 2008.

BENEFITS OF LISTED INFRASTRUCTURE INVESTMENTS

According to institutional investors including pension funds, endowments, foundations, and sovereign wealth funds, top attributes of an attractive infrastructure investment include:

- Diversification
- Liquidity

- Reasonable fees
- Valuation and daily market pricing
- Transparent corporate governance
- Active management and value creation[3]

Listed infrastructure can provide these unique attributes to investors in a framework that can be easy to understand, differentiating it from many other complex, unlisted investments. The following represents a more detailed discussion of the attributes of infrastructure investments.

1. **Diversification.** In the world of finance, diversification is a risk management technique that involves holding a variety of investments within a portfolio. The spreading out of investments across various investments reduces risk. Diversification is the best risk mitigator. Listed infrastructure permits investors to diversify across "sectors," which helps to ameliorate some of the inherent risks that are present in infrastructure. These risks include regulatory risk, demand risk, interest rate, and refinancing risk. Diversification across regulatory sectors, physical assets, currency exposure and political risks (country or regions) helps investors construct a portfolio that achieves their desired risk return profile or "risk budgeting process." This can be achieved in a global diversified portfolio of holdings.

2. **Liquidity.** A large investment universe can provide greater liquidity opportunities. Investors may access investment vehicles, separately managed accounts, and mutual funds—all of which have liquidity that is not available in direct project finance deals. This liquidity feature allows investors to deploy capital and conversely trims their listed infrastructure exposure to maintain their asset allocation models.

3. **Reasonable Fees.** *Fee drag* or the fees and costs that are accessed to an investment portfolio challenges investors and portfolio managers alike when it comes to investment performance. Fees are typically higher in private infrastructure transactions. An actively managed portfolio of listed infrastructure investments at institutional pricing can be more attractive.

4. **Valuation and Daily Market Pricing.** Unlisted infrastructure valuations are performed by an independent auditor or administrator. On the other hand, since listed securities are exchange traded and market priced, investors are provided with the visibility that they need, especially in the current market environment where investment transparency is at a premium.

5. **Transparent Corporate Governance.** Listed companies are subject to examination by regulatory authorities, governments, investor advocacy groups like UNPRI/UN Global Compact, and labor unions, and are

subject to media scrutiny. Today there is an increased focus by these companies on social issues, the environment, and corporate governance.

6. **Active Management and Value Criteria.** The value proposition behind active investments in a portfolio of listed infrastructure securities can be seen through examining the composition of the frequently used benchmarks. The Macquarie Global Infrastructure Benchmark is almost entirely comprised of global-listed utilities companies (approximately 90 percent). The S&P Global Infrastructure Benchmark is a bit more diversified, comprised of 40 percent utilities companies, 40 percent transportation companies, and 20 percent energy companies. Active portfolio management in the listed infrastructure sector provides the ability to generate significant returns while avoiding unwanted sector concentration in the benchmark. Additionally, stock market volatility has risen recently, creating a greater dispersion of returns among individual stocks and expanding the scope for active managers to distinguish themselves from a benchmark.

RISKS AND REWARDS

Investing in listed infrastructure provides the ability for investors to add income, further diversify their portfolio, and thereby improve overall long-term performance. Infrastructure investors add another asset class with a low degree of correlation relative to the other assets in the aggregate portfolio. If history is an indicator, stock market recoveries have come in relatively short bursts and outperformance has occurred in a select number of sectors; infrastructure has been one of these sectors. As the markets continue to rebound from their lows, listed infrastructure is well positioned to capitalize for investors.

Viewing the historical data, infrastructure stocks have typically experienced yields of 5.15 percent, while traditional stocks have yielded 4.37 percent, and bonds have produced yields of 4.29 percent.[4] These securities' yield and growth potential have made infrastructure stocks attractive during economic booms and busts, particularly when compared with the long-term performance characteristics of common stocks and bonds (see Exhibit 10.2).

INVESTMENT OUTLOOK

Global growth dynamics continue to drive investment in infrastructure worldwide. Populations in Latin America, India, China, and southeastern

EXHIBIT 10.2 Infrastructure Stocks Providing Return Enhancement to Stock and Bond Portfolios

	Bonds	Common Stocks	Infrastructure Stocks
Annualized returns	6.52%	0.83%	10.86%
Annualized volatility	5.89%	15.31%	14.95%
Infrastructure correlations	36.44%	85.53%	

Notes: Figures are from November 30, 2001 to December 31, 2008.
Common stocks refer to the S&P Global 1200.
Bonds refer to the Barclays Capital Global Aggregate.
Infrastructure stocks refer to the S&P Global Infrastructure Index.
Sources: Standard & Poor's and Lehman Brothers.

Asia are experiencing infrastructure investment growth over multiple sectors including regulated utilities, transportation, and social infrastructure. This infrastructure investment growth is necessary for these regions to accommodate their explosive population growth (see Exhibit 10.3).

In contrast, examination of the United States and Europe reveals a different story in terms of demographic trends. Economists are beginning to see some of the "green shoots" of economic recovery that are leading them to believe that there is light at the end of the tunnel and it is not a train. Green shoots are the beginnings of renewed growth after the scorched earth that was created by the 2007 and 2008 financial Armageddon. Effects of the $787 billion stimulus package that was implemented in the United States are taking hold and select industries are benefitting from the government services effort. The stimulus total for infrastructure, science, renovation projects for government and educational buildings came to roughly $120 billion.[5]

EXHIBIT 10.3 Global Growth Dynamics Drive Investment

Age	China	India	Mexico	Western Europe	USA
0–19	30.90%	41.30%	41.00%	22.60%	27.70%
20–39	33.50	32.20	32.70	26.60	27.60
40–59	24.80	18.90	18.10	28.70	27.90
60+	10.80	7.65	8.20	22.10	16.80

Source: U.S. Bureau of the Census, International Database, Global Population Report 2007.

Capital Innovations LLC shared the breakdown of this package for a recent *New York Times* article:

- $26.5 billion—Energy investments, including $4.5 billion for retrofitting federal buildings to improve energy efficiency and $11 billion to modernize the electric grid.
- $7.5 billion—Promoting drinking water infrastructure improvements and infrastructure improvements for water and waste disposal in rural areas.
- $6.25 billion—Public housing development and renovation.
- $28.5 billion—Infrastructure improvement, which includes $7.2 billion to increase broadband access and usage.
- $48 billion—Transportation projects, including a $27.5 billion investment in highway improvements and construction and $9.3 billion investment in rail transportation.

Clearly, there are a host of beneficiaries from this package and the benefits will continue to accrue to select organizations throughout 2009. Thus, security selection will remain critical. The developed markets countries need to rebuild and retrofit their existing infrastructure, so these countries will focus on investment in Brownfield (existing infrastructure) and Rehabilitative Brownfield for the foreseeable future. Emerging market countries have a slightly different challenge in that these target regions need to build infrastructure from the ground up. Therefore, Greenfield or new infrastructure projects and companies will be the area of highest growth for these developing nations.

From an economic perspective, there are concerns regarding short-term deflation and much more widespread fears of long-term, worldwide inflation. The exposure to a diversified pool of infrastructure securities has shown beneficial to investors in both scenarios. In the post-2008 credit crisis, short-term deflation has proven to be a pervasive determinant, creating a difficult market in which to operate or invest. Falling consumer prices in the first half of 2009 and excessive market volatility have further hindered investors seeking shelter from the storm. The market, as a whole, is extremely tumultuous and volatile, offering the opportunity for either outperformance or underperformance (see Exhibit 10.4).

Where we are headed? The stimulus package and additional money have been injected into the U.S. financial system, leading investors to the next big challenge: a rising inflationary environment. Many members of Wall Street's "old guard" have previously witnessed this type of environment in the 1970s. This year, in hopes of staving off the effects of deflation, these investors have piled into bonds and real estate, and begun to invest

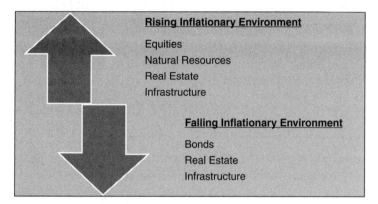

EXHIBIT 10.4 Infrastructure Asset Class Performance in Various Markets
Source: Capital Innovations, LLC.

in infrastructure. Investors are now faced with a common predicament: how to position themselves for this swing in inflation without tactically reallocating too much of the portfolio. To respond to this challenge, institutional investors, investment consultants, and retail investors are committing double-digit figures of their portfolios to four specific asset classes: equities, natural resources, real estate, and infrastructure securities. These asset classes will act as a hedgelike instrument toward the effects of increasing prices or inflation "shock" over the next three to five years, adjusting with prices increases and helping to mitigate the effects of the inflation bubble on portfolios.

Capital Innovations LLC continues to actively monitor the global infrastructure market. We believe that Europe is currently restructuring its banking system. Large-scale banking woes in Western Europe have been augmented by the spillover effect from Eastern European financial institutions, many of which have bled into their balance sheets. These institutions will take a considerable amount of time to be purged from the greater European financial system, causing the sovereign debt of numerous European countries and currencies to face significant problems in 2010 and beyond. Investment professionals continue to focus their attention on U.S. investment opportunities, with a bias toward companies with a global footprint.

Investors will look for companies that have the ability to hedge the currency risk as well as negotiate long-term contracts that generate the inelastic revenue streams that institutional investors find attractive during these times of growing inflation and uncertainty.

During this period of increased volatility, investors are struggling to find reliable asset classes that offer the potential for dependable, long lasting performance and short term liquidity. Infrastructure investments offer protection from inflation, inelastic demand, and stable cash flows. Listed infrastructure offers investors the chance to capitalize on all the advantages of the asset class within a liquid investment vehicle through direct security ownership or professionally managed funds.

ENDNOTES

1. Standard & Poor's. "Listed Infrastructure Assets—A Primer, A Short Guide to Listed Infrastructure Investing and the S&P Global Infrastructure Index." March 18, 2009. http://www2.standardandpoors.com/spf/pdf/index/Gbl-Infrastructure_Primer.pdf.
2. Report Card for America's Infrastructure 2009, American Society of Civil Engineers, January 28, 2009. www.asce.org/reportcard/2009/grades.cfm. Accessed November 20, 2009.
3. Capital Innovations LLC, Institutional Investor Survey, October 2009.
4. Standard & Poor's, Lehman Brothers yields for common stocks are for the S&P Global 1200. www.standardandpoors.com/indices/sp-global-1200/en/us/?indexId=spgcmp1200usdff-p-rgll-. Accessed November 20, 2009. Yields for bonds are for the Lehman Global Aggregate Index: www.lehman.com/fi/indices/pdf/Global_Aggregate_Index.pdf. Yields for listed infrastructure assets are for the S&P Global Infrastructure index: www.standardandpoors.com/indices/sp-global-infrastructure/en/us/?indexId=spgbthini-usdw-p-rgl-. Data as of November 30, 2008.
5. American Recovery and Reinvestment Act of 2009. http://appropriations.house.gov/pdf/RecoveryBill01-15-09.pdf, 1/6/2009. Accessed November 19, 2009.

Institutional Infrastructure Program Management

Michael D. Underhill
Founder, Capital Innovations LLC

Managing an institutional infrastructure investment program for a corporate pension plan, public retirement program, or massive sovereign wealth fund is no small task. Institutional investors need to be cognizant of multiple issues: extensive program design, portfolio planning, asset allocation, diversification, risk management, portfolio management, monitoring, and reporting that may span multiple investment vehicles.

The first step toward building an investment program is designing a policy that will guide it and ensure an appropriate fit with other asset classes in their overall investment program. This policy also must fit with any existing inflation-linked investments (Treasury Inflation-Protected Securities, Commodities, Timber, Agriculture, etc.) in order to be successful. Defining the infrastructure asset class to include a range of sectors, return assumptions, investment vehicles or types, incorporating risk management systems while keeping in mind any type of special collateral investment objective (union labor or social screens) is critical during the design phase. Institutional investors' infrastructure investment policy statement (IIPS) should include but not be limited to:

- A stated allocation percentage, typically ranging from 5 percent to 7 percent but allowable up to 10 percent depending on the overall asset allocation or risk budget of the fund
- A target for an average annual investment return, typically 500 basis points over the rate of inflation, net of fees, over a five-year investment time horizon

- Vehicles: public and private infrastructure securities, including funds and direct investments
- Sectors: transportation, energy, natural resources, utilities, water, communications, and other social support services

The ability to construct a cogent investment thesis that incorporates multiple dimensions of risk management in a framework that enhances the portfolio manager and investment committee's ability to manage risk is an institutional investor's best defense against poor investment performance. Working with institutional investors and sovereign wealth funds over the course of my career has shown me that flexibility, control, and responsiveness are keys to managing large institutional pools of capital effectively. It is particularly pertinent in the dynamic market environment that has become professional money management today as things change often.

An infrastructure investment program should have stated objectives or goals, which should incorporate attaining long-term returns against a stated benchmark or set of benchmarks. Unlisted infrastructure investments have few relevant benchmarks, but as an industry standard, core infrastructure investment returns are typically benchmarked against the consumer price index (CPI) plus 300 to 500 basis points, depending on how much leverage is involved in the investment. Core infrastructure investment definitions typically cover mature operating assets that provide stable cash flow, long-term monopoly positions, and a significant cash yield. Core, established Brownfield infrastructure assets with little or no financial leverage and long-term off-take agreements that help to generate long-term stable cash flow should generate target returns in the 10 percent to 12 percent range. That being said, if there are Brownfield assets that are highly leveraged transactions, one must budget for that additional risk and factor it in according to the benchmarking process.

Value-added unlisted infrastructure investment returns are typically benchmarked against the CPI[1] plus 500 basis points or the Ten Year U.S. Treasury Index. Value-added assets are less mature, operating assets that may be poised for a growth phase that would provide for a higher return potential. Returns may be generated in a variety of ways from these types of investments, but an investor must be careful that investment performance attribution is performed on prior comparable investments to ascertain how returns will be generated. Financial engineering (leverage), operational improvement, and, more typically, a combination of those two are utilized to generate returns in these types of investments. Knowing the difference between financial engineering and operational improvement and measuring the amount appropriately means the program can be run more efficiently and effectively.

Opportunistic unlisted infrastructure investments involve an increased level of risk and return potential for investors, Greenfield development and construction provide for this higher degree of risk and should be risk budgeted accordingly. Benchmarking against the CPI^2 plus 500 basis points or the Ten Year U.S. Treasury Index is a starting point, but one must adhere to the standards of the prudent investor act when considering any investment that is classified as opportunistic.

That being said, there is not yet a perfect benchmark for unlisted infrastructure that serves as a relevant proxy for all of the investment types (core, value-added, and opportunistic). And the industry is not close to finding one. There just haven't been many investment realizations in U.S. infrastructure and the current market environment with exit opportunities lacking in other geographic regions is also a factor. Capital Innovations LLC has created customized benchmarks for a number of large institutional clients, but these were created on a case-by-case basis.

Listed infrastructure investments in the portfolio may be benchmarked to the S&P Global Infrastructure Index as it is one of the more robust global benchmarks for marketable listed infrastructure investments. It consists of three different segments: Approximately 40 percent of the index investments are in the transportation sector, 40 percent in utilities, and 20 percent in energy investments. Alternatively, the Macquarie Global Infrastructure Index may be used, which is comprised of roughly 90 percent global utilities. It should be noted that listed infrastructure possesses a unique attribute in providing liquidity, but with that liquidity also comes market beta or public markets volatility that needs to be factored into the benchmarking, portfolio management, and risk management equation.

Another program goal should be preservation of capital with the intention of the underlying investments to provide cash flow and potential for modest capital appreciation without assuming undue risk, which is easier said than done. The portfolio manager and investment committee's ability to identify quality investment opportunities and transact on them in a timely manner is predicated on the ability to gauge risk and return on a case-by-case basis and act accordingly.

Setting parameters for the overall infrastructure investment portfolio will help to adjust ("dial up" or "dial down") the risk ranges using a series of portfolio metrics as risk adjustment devices. Diversifying the portfolio across various geographies in unlisted and listed infrastructure can provide varying degrees of risk from stable, developed markets to higher risk, emerging markets geographies. This will generate various levels of risk that can help fine-tune the portfolio to achieve the appropriate risk budget sought by the infrastructure program's investment policy statement. Another set of risk metrics that may be utilized across unlisted and listed infrastructure are

Highly regulated   **Less regulated**

Less competitive   **More competitive**

Social Infrastructure	Regulated Assets	User Pay Assets	Competitive Assets
• Courts • Hospitals • Schools • Law Enforcement and Military	• Transmission Assets • Distribution Assets • Water and Sewage	• Road • Rail • Airports	• Certain Communications Infrastructure • Certain Power Infrastructure • Energy Trading

Increasing Risk

EXHIBIT 11.1 Risk and Regulatory Framework
Source: Michael Underhill; source data: Macquarie Research, 2007.

infrastructure subsectors: transportation, energy, utilities, water, communications, and other social support services. As can be seen in Exhibit 11.1, risk and the regulatory framework go hand in hand when evaluating the appropriateness of an investment for the portfolio.

A portfolio manager can only manage what one can measure consistently and systematically. Application of a *risk register* to measure standardized criteria across infrastructure investments further sharpens a portfolio manager's and investment committee's ability to quantify risk and confirm that the risks associated with the investment are consistent with the investment program's stated objectives. Identifying all of the risks and recording them in the investment program's risk register is an important step toward appropriate risk management for any institutional investor. Infrastructure investment program risk spans a broad continuum that may cover: credit risk, currency risk, political risk and public risk, labor risk, regulatory risk, construction risk, market risk, environmental risk or climate risk, financial risk for investments that may employ substantial leverage (borrowing), liquidity risk for unlisted investments that have time horizons greater than 10 years, country or geographic region risk, structural risk, or valuation risk.

Taking the comprehensive assessment and then building an asset allocation framework that incorporates concentration limits on geographies, diversification limits by subsectors, limits on any single investment in a security (listed or unlisted) with appropriate equity and debt limits will help to define investment parameters in the program. These measures will help to ameliorate risk and optimize return by further diversifying the investment program or pool ensuring that there are appropriate hedges against inflation risk as well.

Designing the program to invest capital over a specified time period helps to further diversify investment risk in a manner similar to *dollar cost averaging into the market*. This can be done with both unlisted and listed infrastructure investments over a period of months or even may take years for some larger state pension fund investments pools or sovereign wealth funds. Unlisted infrastructure parlance refers to this as *vintage year* diversification, which may help to ensure that an investor does not deploy all of his capital in a time period when valuations for unlisted infrastructure are exceptionally high and one would be buying in at the height of the market. It also helps mitigate effects of unexpected events such as a credit crisis, oil shock, or any financial shock.

UNLISTED INFRASTRUCTURE SECURITY SELECTION

The process for identifying appropriate investments can be a daunting challenge for institutional investors of any size. Unlisted infrastructure involves a greater degree of complexities as the market is more opaque to an outsider or untrained eye and gaining access to truly high quality deal flow is difficult. The quality deals find capital at varying velocities, the great deals require reconnaissance, diligence, judgment, and at times, a proprietary skill set to identify and transact in the more specialized sectors of the unlisted infrastructure market. There is an abundance of deal flow presently due to the global financial crisis, inadequately structured leverage, and forced sellers giving up assets for sometimes pennies on the dollar. These infrastructure assets are not distressed, the sellers are financially distressed due to overextension or aggressive business practices during the infrastructure investment bubble in 2007 and 2008. The investment environment will continue to be attractive for quite some time as companies are pressed to deleverage and unwind their positions. The combination of distressed sellers and dismal budgetary situation of local governments will provide a once-in-a-lifetime opportunity to build a portfolio of unlisted infrastructure investments at rock bottom valuations.

BUILD AMERICA BONDS

A notable infrastructure opportunity set that has arrived on the scene recently are Build America Bonds. The U.S. Treasury implemented the Build

America Bond program under the American Recovery and Reinvestment Act of 2009 to provide funding for state and local governments at lower borrowing costs. This program was designed to enable state and local governments to pursue necessary capital projects, such as work on public buildings, courthouses, schools, roads, transportation infrastructure, government hospitals, public safety facilities and equipment, water and sewer projects, environmental projects, energy projects, governmental housing projects and public utilities. Traditionally, tax-exempt bonds provide a critical source of capital for state and local governments, but the recession reduced their ability to finance new projects. Supplementing this existing market, the Build America Bond program is designed to provide a federal subsidy for a larger portion of the borrowing costs of state and local governments than traditional tax-exempt bonds in order to stimulate the economy and encourage investments in capital projects in 2009 and 2010.[3]

These securities need to be considered as they are well suited for institutional investors seeking fixed-income returns offering municipal credit quality at corporate-equivalent yields. Taxable bond issuance has exploded by 115 percent in 2009 and of the $48.2 billion of taxable bonds sold thus far in 2009, over $33 billion consists of Build America Bonds. According to the Investment Company Institute, long-term, tax-exempt mutual funds have received net cash flows of $44.6 billion during the first eight months of 2009 (not including reinvested dividends of $7.9 billion). When compared to an annual rate of growth in tax-exempt mutual fund assets of $14.7 billion per year from 1998 to 2008, it is obvious that both institutional and retail investors have been and will continue to be attracted to this new and innovative investment structure.

LISTED INFRASTRUCTURE EQUITIES

Listed infrastructure equity securities offer investors the ability to participate in a global basket of securities that span multiple sectors: the energy sector (oil and gas storage, oil and gas transportation); transportation sector (airport services, highways and rail tracks, marine ports and services), and utilities (electric utilities, multi utilities, gas utilities and water utilities). These sectors inherently have different risk and return characteristics with risk and return profiles further differentiated across multiple geographies and currencies. Listed infrastructure provides investors with transparency and governance provisions that make it easier for investors to conduct due diligence and assess performance, so naturally it has been more popular in its applications for institutional and retail investors. We have seen institutional investors implement asset allocations models that have allocated a top down

3 to 5 percent of overall portfolio exposure to listed infrastructure as a way to gain exposure to the return of the asset class while maintaining a degree of liquidity during uncertain times. Recently with the global financial crisis and excessive use of leverage in unlisted infrastructure funds, listed infrastructure has become the method of choice for infrastructure allocations of significant institutional entities as well as high net worth investors.

The ability to optimize investment performance and ensure proper fit for the investment program varies across listed and unlisted infrastructure. Listed infrastructure securities are a bit less problematic when it comes to portfolio management because these types of securities are liquid and can be redeemed or traded in the market. The more challenging side of infrastructure program portfolio management involves unlisted private fund investments or direct infrastructure deals because the critical issue is to make an investment work *after* it has been selected.

PORTFOLIO MONITORING

After capital is invested, portfolio performance monitoring tools are critical to evaluating performance against the relevant listed infrastructure and unlisted infrastructure benchmark. This is a systematic framework that will help identify any problematic accounts early so that these investments may be addressed and action may be taken. Monitoring systems for unlisted infrastructure investments and listed infrastructure investments are very different. Unlisted infrastructure valuation, monitoring, and reporting is more akin to private equity or private real estate-type reporting, involving independent valuation or independent appraisals formally on a quarterly basis. Identifying problems in the unlisted segment of the portfolio is a bit more challenging as the unlisted portfolio investment snapshot is only taken once a financial quarter formally or a few times intraquarter but there are monitoring systems and technology that are advancing rapidly that allow investors to gain more frequent updates on portfolio valuations and developments. Valuation methodologies for unlisted infrastructure are covered in Chapter 9.

Institutional portfolio management requires a combination of monitoring, communications, and ongoing due diligence with all of the investment professionals involved in the program. Frequent updates provide a view of the program but managing an infrastructure program using a rearview mirror approach or past performance statement is not advised. Constant surveillance of the unlisted and listed infrastructure markets and ongoing intelligence is required to meet the demands of the program and ensure operational efficiency. The ability of a portfolio manager or investment committee to act in a judicious manner will help your program perform according to your stated objectives and guide the program toward successful returns for its beneficiaries for years to come.

ENDNOTES

1. Prior month trailing 12-month U.S. Consumer Price Index, all urban consumers, not seasonally adjusted.
2. Ibid.
3. U.S. Treasury Department, April 2009. www.treas.gov/press/releases/docs/ BuildAmericaandSchoolConstructionBondsFactsheetFinal.pdf.

CHAPTER 12

Legal Aspects of Infrastructure Investments

Joseph Seliga
Partner, Mayer Brown

T he United States often is described as a "nation of laws." This is especially true in the area of infrastructure investment. The multiplicity of governmental entities at the federal, state, and local levels results in an overlapping patchwork of laws that impacts all aspects of a transaction. This chapter describes the interplay of these federal, state, and local laws and the unique effects they have on infrastructure transactions in the United States.

THE GROWTH OF PRIVATE INVESTMENT IN U.S. INFRASTRUCTURE

While public-private partnerships (PPPs) in infrastructure have a long history in the United States going back to the construction and operation of turnpikes, canals, and railroads in the early years of the country, during the first decade of the 21st century, a renewed focus has developed on the benefits of private investment in U.S. infrastructure. This development is related to a number of factors. First, and most important, the infrastructure needs of the United States are great and the financial resources to address those needs are lacking. Private investment offers an opportunity for governments to tap into new sources of infrastructure capital. In addition, private investment in infrastructure brings the benefits of private operation and with it efficiency, innovation, and cost savings. At the same time, the growth of private investment in infrastructure in other parts of the world has led to the creation of a multitude of international companies with experience in construction, operation, and maintenance of infrastructure, numerous equity investors willing to invest in attractive projects, and an established market of international banks familiar with infrastructure investment, all of which have been eager to become active in the United States.

These developments have led to a series of transactions involving investment in existing infrastructure and the development of new infrastructure in the United States in various different sectors, including roads and bridges, parking, airports, and ports. In the existing infrastructure area, the capacity for a U.S. market has been demonstrated through the $1.83 billion long-term concession of the Chicago Skyway Toll Bridge, the $3.8 billion long-term concession of the Indiana Toll Road, the $611 million concession of the Pocahontas Parkway in Virginia, the $603 million concession of the Northwest Parkway in Colorado, the $563 million concession of the Chicago downtown underground parking system, the $1.157 billion concession of Chicago's metered parking system, the long-term concession of several container terminals by the Port of Oakland and a recent $8.9 billion unsolicited proposal to enter into a long-term PPP related to the operations of the Port of Virginia. Two other path-breaking transactions achieved binding bids but did not close as a result of different factors: the $12.8 billion proposed concession of the Pennsylvania Turnpike, which did not close because the Pennsylvania legislature ultimately did not adopt authorizing legislation, and the $2.521 billion proposed concession of Chicago Midway International Airport, which was not able to reach financial close as a result of the effects of the global economic downturn in late 2008 and early 2009. The binding bids achieved with respect to both of these transactions, however, demonstrate the significant interest that has developed in the infrastructure asset class.

At the same time as these developments have occurred in the area of existing infrastructure, numerous states and local governments have engaged with the private sector to develop new infrastructure. Various state and local agencies in Texas have developed new toll roads through PPPs, including concessions under which the private sector constructs and develops a highway project, then recoups its investment with a certain return through toll revenues it obtains while it operates the project. The Dulles Greenway project in Virginia was constructed and is operated as a privately owned toll road subject to public utility regulation by the Commonwealth of Virginia. The Capital Beltway high-occupancy toll lane project is being developed in Virginia as an over $1 billion long-term concession. The Florida Department of Transportation's I-595 managed lanes transaction was the first availability payment transaction in the United States, a transaction in which the private sector finances the project, but tolls and associated revenue risk are retained by the government, with the government responsible for making payments to the private sector if the project is completed on schedule and is operated and maintained according to certain contract requirements. North Carolina and Mississippi are in the process of procuring the first toll projects in their states through PPPs. Rapid transit agencies in Oakland, Denver, and Dallas are procuring new mass transit projects through PPPs as well.

These transactions described are based in some ways on international precedents given the established state of the market abroad, but in many other ways they are distinctly American. As a general matter, under the federal system of the United States, the development and operation of infrastructure is largely a matter left to state governments with those state governments giving responsibility for large portions of infrastructure to local governments, sometimes to counties, cities, towns, and villages and in other cases to specific local government authorities, such as highway, airport, parking, mass transit and port authorities. This structure results in a variety of unique legal issues that have a significant effect on various aspects of infrastructure transactions, including authorization and process, mandatory legal requirements, and ongoing operations.

VARYING SOURCES OF STATE AND LOCAL AUTHORITY TO UNDERTAKE TRANSACTIONS

As a general matter, infrastructure investment transactions involving public assets require some type of legal authorization. If the asset is under the jurisdiction of a state agency, typically the state will adopt authorizing legislation that enables that agency to enter into transactions involving private investment. Roughly half of the states have adopted this type of legislation, but the forms vary widely. The legislation could be written in general terms, permitting transactions, both through solicited and unsolicited proposals, to be undertaken with respect to any type of transportation asset, subject to certain process elements being followed. Virginia's authorizing legislation is an example of this approach. Or the legislation could be more specific in nature, such as Indiana's legislation authorizing the Indiana Toll Road transaction, which was specific to that transaction and another proposed transaction related to the development of a new road in southern and central Indiana. There is a range of alternatives in between, including legislation confined to specific types of assets (highways and bridges only, for instance), specific types of transactions (only existing asset or new asset development transactions, for example), and specific types of authorization (preauthorizing transactions if they are undertaken in a manner consistent with the legislation or authorizing a specific negotiated transaction).

Separate authorization issues apply at the local level. Local governments are subject to their own requirements related to authorization of infrastructure transactions. At a basic level, the local government must have a source of authority for the transaction from the state level. This is typically achieved in one of two ways. Certain states have adopted the concept of municipal "home rule" under which all or certain local governments have general authority for their own affairs so long as those affairs are not a matter of statewide concern or the authority is otherwise preempted by the state. In states where "home rule" does not apply or in the case of local governments not subject to "home rule," the state legislature must grant specific legislative authorization for a transaction. This can be provided in the same manner as those transactions undertaken by state agencies. Some local government agencies, particularly special purpose transportation authorities have pre-existing authorizing legislation that is broad enough to include the grant to enter into transactions involving private investment. In addition to the grant of state authority to undertake a transaction, local governments typically have a process for approval of a transaction by the governmental entity. Often, this approval will take the form of the review and approval of a specific contract after it has been negotiated. This is the process that has been undertaken with respect to a number of a large infrastructure transactions by local governments in the United States, such as the city of Chicago, which has undertaken its infrastructure transactions pursuant to its home rule authority but has had the specific contracts for each transaction approved by its city council and the Northwest Parkway Public Highway Authority in Colorado, which undertook its concession of the Northwest Parkway under the state legislation authorizing the creation of the authority and had its specific contract for the concession of the parkway approved by its board of directors.

Ultimately, for a transaction to be undertaken, a sufficient source of authorization must exist and that authorization must enable the governmental entity not only to undertake the transaction but to carry out its obligations in the project documents. States are subject to sovereign immunity from claims against them unless that immunity is otherwise waived. In some states, local governments have the benefit of sovereign immunity. Together with the fundamental issue of whether a transaction is authorized, another fundamental issue is whether the governmental entity benefits from immunity and, if so, whether that immunity is waived or an effective alternative mechanism is established to ensure that the contracting party in an infrastructure transaction has an effective means of bringing suit and obtaining damages from the governmental entity in the event the governmental entity breaches its contractual obligations. A related fundamental issue is the ability to obtain funds from the governmental entity after a successful claim has been brought against the governmental entity. This concept, referred to as *appropriations risk*, is common when contracting with governmental entities and often is an accepted element of contracting with a governmental party so long as the contracting party has assurance that the risk is mitigated to the maximum extent possible through authorizing legislation and the project documents.

DIFFERENT GOVERNMENTS, DIFFERENT TRANSACTION PROCESSES

The manner in which a transaction is authorized can have a significant effect on process elements. State legislation authorizing infrastructure transactions may set forth specific process requirements, including in some cases, requirements to have transactions approved in concept before they are undertaken, to hold public hearings before or during a transaction process or to comply with approval requirements or review periods after a transaction is negotiated but before project documents are executed or a transaction is closed. In other cases, state agencies are given greater latitude to undertake transaction processes as they deem appropriate. In addition, local governments with a source of authority to undertake transactions usually have greater flexibility to establish process elements. Most transactions undertaken in the U.S. market, both involving existing assets and new construction projects, have followed a two-part process. First, the request for qualifications is issued to obtain responses from potential private sector partners. Then, the government makes a determination of what respondents are considered qualified to move forward and then begins a procurement process with a final decision to enter into a transaction dependent on what respondent submits the highest offer in the case of existing assets or what respondent submits the best value proposal in the case of new construction assets. Another variable would be to select the proposer that imposes the lowest tolls or the shortest term, although these structures have not yet been utilized in the U.S. market. In some cases, governments have chosen to enter into exclusive negotiations with a selected respondent after offers or proposals are submitted in an effort to achieve higher or better value. Some governments have included the concept of a public sector comparator, derived from processes established in other parts of the world, to determine if private investment would achieve a better result than the public sector would in undertaking the same project.

GOVERNMENT CONTRACTING REQUIREMENTS PROMOTING STATE AND LOCAL POLICY OBJECTIVES

While the terms of legislative authorization can have an impact on process elements of a transaction, they also can have an effect on mandatory legal requirements related to a transaction. The terms of legislative authorization could impose specific government contract requirements that could include compliance with minority, women, disabled or veterans contracting goals, prevailing wage and living wage requirements, employee residence goals, disclosure requirements (including those related to ownership and possibly activities such as investments in certain countries or past historical practices, such as involvement in the slave trade), labor provisions related to existing employees and new employees and interoperability requirements in the case of tolling equipment.

In some cases, while state legislative authorization may not be necessary for a specific transaction, it may be necessary for elements of a transaction. For example, in the case of transactions undertaken by the city of Chicago, state law in Illinois requires that private entities that lease land owned by governmental entities must pay property taxes on their leasehold interest as if they were the owner of the property unless a legislative exception applies. This would make transactions involving private investment in infrastructure financially prohibitive. As a result, while the city of Chicago did not need legislative authorization to enter into its infrastructure transactions, it did need to seek state legislation exceptions from the leasehold property tax. In the case of the City's proposed transaction related to Chicago Midway International Airport, the legislation authorizing the property tax exemption also includes requirements related to the transaction that limited expansion of the airport in the residential area where the airport is located and that require that the private contracting party make offers to existing airport employees, comply with labor neutrality and card check procedures and provide wages and benefits consistent with those provided to union employees at the airport prior to the transaction. The legislation also includes requirements as to how the City of Chicago is to spend proceeds from the transaction, including requirements that at least 90 percent be spent on municipal infrastructure projects or contributions to municipal employee pension plans and that infrastructure projects funded from such proceeds are subject to project labor agreement requirements.

As this brief summary indicates, the types of mandatory contracting requirements that may be imposed by state and local governments can vary significantly depending on the governmental entity involved and specific state and local policy objectives. It is a critical element for governments undertaking transactions to determine what requirements should apply to a transaction, for contracting parties to understand these requirements and for both parties to consider what effect they may have on a potential transaction.

In addition, it is critical for governments and for private investors to consider what rights governmental entities with jurisdiction over a project (whether they are parties to a contract) should have on an ongoing basis with respect to an asset. This includes additional governmental operating requirements, the development of competing facilities, and the enactment of new laws. The long-term concession structure (often with a leasehold interest in which the government continues to retain property rights) presumes an active ongoing contractual role of the procuring governmental entity through the imposition of construction and operating standards, ongoing capital improvement requirements, government access and monitoring provisions, and emergency override provisions. However, contracts typically provide for compensation, and in some cases, termination rights, for the private entity when the procuring government entity (and possibly other state or local governmental agencies) impose requirements that are arbitrary or discriminatory or undertake certain activities not fundamental to the government's oversight rights that are not otherwise permitted under the contract.

THE FEDERAL ROLE: LIMITED BUT CRITICAL

As I described, the federal role related to infrastructure transactions in the United States, while critically important, is typically limited to certain transaction elements. Project documents include general requirements to apply with federal laws, such as environmental laws, security regulations, and specific laws and regulations related to the asset class as applicable. Transactions, however, usually are not subject to federal approval, except that certain aspects of federal approvals may apply. For example, foreign involvement in a transaction may be subject to approval by the Committee on Foreign Investment in the United States (CFIUS), if the transaction involves certain types of foreign investment or the investor plans to hire a foreign-based operator. Typically, though, federal involvement in a transaction process is limited to issues related to federal funding or financing, which could involve the prior use of federal funding for a specific asset or the use of federal financing assistance for a transaction or the continued use of federal funding for an asset. In the case of existing highway projects, for instance, if federal funding has been used for an asset, the asset may be subject to a federal funding agreement that may need to be reviewed in relation to the transaction. In the case of airports, for example, federal law does not allow proceeds of a transaction involving the privatization of a federally funded airport to be used other than for airport purposes. However, a federal law authorizes the privatization of a limited number of airports and the ability to take proceeds "off the airport system" if the transaction complies with certain requirements, including certain airline approval requirements and approval by the Federal Aviation Administration (FAA).

Several programs have been created under federal law that provide financing assistance for transactions involving private investment. For example, federal law permits the use of private activity bonds for certain surface transportation projects, enabling state or local governments to issue municipal debt at tax-exempt rates for privately constructed or operated projects. In addition, the Transportation Infrastructure Finance and Innovation Act (TIFIA), provides federal credit assistance in the form of low-interest subordinated loans, loan guarantees and letters of credit, for surface transportation projects. These projects have been created to help create a more level playing field between projects involving public financing that can as a matter of law benefit from the issuance of tax-exempt debt and projects involving private investment. When TIFIA or private-activity bond financing applies to a project certain additional federal requirements may apply. For example, projects receiving TIFIA assistance are subject to the National Environmental Policy Act (NEPA), which includes an environmental review process and the possibility of the issuance of an environmental impact statement after a public comment period if the project is determined to have a significant impact on the environment.

The United States is a dynamic market for infrastructure investment with numerous opportunities related to existing assets and new asset development. To maximize the benefits of private investment in U.S. infrastructure, state and local governments need to develop an understanding of the infrastructure market, to undertake transactions that are well suited to private investment and to develop processes that are worth the investment of private sector resources. On the other hand, to tap into the U.S. market most effectively, private sector investors need to understand the differing objectives of state and local governments in the United States and the variety of unique federal, state, and local legal aspects of partnering with governmental entities. As this mutual understanding continues to develop, the opportunities from private investment in infrastructure both for investors and governmental entities will grow.